Teaching Science in Elementary Schools

D1528819

Teaching Science in Elementary Schools

50 Dynamic Activities That Encourage Student Interest in Science

S. Kay Gandy
Harmony Hendrick
Jessica Roberts

ROWMAN & LITTLEFIELD
Lanham • Boulder • New York • London

Published by Rowman & Littlefield
An imprint of The Rowman & Littlefield Publishing Group, Inc.
4501 Forbes Boulevard, Suite 200, Lanham, Maryland 20706
www.rowman.com
86-90 Paul Street, London EC2A 4NE, United Kingdom

British Library Cataloguing in Publication Information Available

Library of Congress Cataloging-in-Publication Data

Names: Gandy, S. Kay, 1954– author. | Hendrick, Harmony, author. | Roberts, Jessica
(Elementary school teacher), author.
Title: Teaching science in elementary schools : 50 dynamic activities that encourage
student interest in science / S. Kay Gandy, Harmony Hendrick, Jessica Roberts.
Description: Lanham, Maryland : Rowman & Littlefield, 2023. | Includes bibliographical
references. | Summary: "The goal of this book is to provide dynamic activities to help
encourage student interest in science, provide quick and easy ideas for teachers, and
supplement content available in the classroom"— Provided by publisher.
Identifiers: LCCN 2023012536 (print) | LCCN 2023012537 (ebook) | ISBN
9781475873092 (cloth) | ISBN 9781475873108 (paperback) | ISBN
9781475873115 (epub)
Subjects: LCSH: Science—Study and teaching (Elementary)—Activity programs.
Classification: LCC LB1585 .G26 2023 (print) | LCC LB1585 (ebook) | DDC
372.35—dc23/eng/20230403
LC record available at https://lccn.loc.gov/2023012536
LC ebook record available at https://lccn.loc.gov/2023012537

Contents

Preface

As a veteran teacher in a very poor school district in Louisiana, the first author learned early in her career to use ordinary, inexpensive materials in the classroom. She spent a lot of time at flea markets and rummage sales looking for anything that could be used as a resource to teach. During her teacher training, she was only required to take two science content courses and one science methods class, so she felt woefully underprepared to teach science.

This is typical of many education programs. It is no wonder that teachers depend upon textbooks to guide their teaching. Unfortunately, science textbooks are not adopted yearly. One science textbook early in the teaching career of the first author stated, "One day, man will go to the moon." It was at this time that the *Challenger* was ready to take the first teacher to space. It is years with no budget to buy school supplies and inadequate, out-of-date science information that prompted the authors to write this book.

This book presents ways to help experienced and novice teachers teach science, without expensive lab equipment. All of the authors are classroom teachers with more than seventy-five combined years of experience between them. The authors believe that these ideas will be exciting and practical for all elementary science teachers.

The authors would especially like to thank the illustrator, Madalyn Stack. She drew the illustrations for this book and the first author's two previous books, *Mapping Is Elementary, My Dear: 100 Activities for Teaching Map Skills to K–6 Students* and *50 Ways to Teach Social Studies for Elementary Teachers*. Madalyn was exceptional in taking vague ideas and developing illustrations of exactly what was needed. Although she was only a young college student with her early work, Madalyn exhibited the highest sense of professionalism in all her endeavors.

The authors would also like to thank all the readers and reviewers for the book and appreciate the input and advice given to make this a better publication. Special thanks to Kathi Matthew, Jeanine Huss, and Anna Nicholas.

Introduction

Children are innately curious about the world when they enter school. Since the goal of science is to understand the natural world, it is imperative that we include student experiences in the science classroom. Since observation and discovery are important elements of learning in the science world, the elementary science class can foster curiosity and learning through questions and activities. In some schools, science is alternated with the teaching of social studies, limiting the amount of time and content that students actually get to learn science. In many schools, science is taught directly from a textbook. The goal of this book is to provide dynamic activities to help encourage student interest in science, provide quick and easy ideas for teachers, and supplement content available in the classroom.

To create an active learning environment, every elementary science classroom can include discovery materials available for student use. Many of these can be secured through donations or bought cheaply at stores or flea markets. Some practical and inexpensive tools include:[1]

- Magnifying glasses
- Binoculars
- Compasses
- Various types of scales
- Magnets
- Assorted sizes of plastic containers with lids
- Assorted funnels, sieves, and sifters
- Rulers and yardsticks
- Timers and stopwatches
- Measuring spoons and cups
- Small nets
- Thermometers
- Hand tools (trowels and shovels)
- Boxes, tubs, and trays

- Prisms
- Pulleys and wheels
- Nuts and bolts
- Gears
- Locks and keys
- Twine
- Gardening gloves
- Camera
- First aid kit
- Bug spray
- Field guides
- Journals
- Disposable eyedroppers

Students learn through creative modes of exploration and inquiry and experimental opportunities provided by knowledgeable teachers. Scientific inquiry helps children understand concepts, such as why water evaporates, why hurricanes develop over the ocean, how electricity works, and the effect of cleanliness on disease prevention. Armed with scientific knowledge, students will be the ones who solve the problems that plague our world in the future. Science knowledge can prepare students to become our future mechanics, electricians, biologists, technicians, architects, and astronauts. With the basic tools of inquiry in hand, students will have an understanding of how the world works.[2]

A basic focus at the elementary level is to teach the scientific method. There are six steps[3] that students can follow:

1. Ask a question to determine what you want to learn about.
2. Gather information and conduct observations.
3. Form a hypothesis (educated guess) about what might happen.
4. Test the hypothesis with an experiment.
5. Analyze the results.
6. Draw conclusions and share with others.

Some common examples of simple experiments that students can use the scientific method to study include: determining if objects will sink or float, creating static electricity with balloons, and demonstrating a volcanic eruption with baking soda and vinegar. Students are more likely to retain information if they are involved in the experiments.[4]

A great way to involve students in learning science is by hosting a science fair. Assign groups, pairs, or individual students a topic. Have students write a project statement in the form of a question to be investigated and then develop a hypothesis about what they think the answer might be. On a trifold board, students will display the results of their research. Have students develop a title that incites curiosity and interest. Other information posted should include: the step-by-step procedures involved in conducting the experiment, variables in the investigation, data displayed in graphs and charts, photographs, results of the experiment, and a conclusion statement.[5] Ask a panel of judges to rate the projects as they ask questions of students during the project presentations.

Science can easily be integrated across other curricula. By making connections with other disciplines, teachers save planning time, reinforce skills, and strengthen content. The essential skills of English language arts (reading, speaking, listening, writing) connect with gathering evidence, analyzing concepts, making arguments, and assessing solutions in science. Teachers can assign journaling in the science class to document what was learned, draw observations, label diagrams, interpret evidence, and even note personal reflections.

Mathematics can be brought into the science classroom by having students visualize and identify patterns in nature, analyze data, measure solutions, or graph results of experiments. Geographical and historical phenomena correlate with science through the study of habitats, food supplies, and the effect of weather patterns on communities. Art can be integrated with science through drawing, painting, sketching, and crafting. There are vast possibilities for the integration of science and other subjects.[6]

Teachers' exposure to formal science courses are often limited to no more than two courses during teacher training, which may limit their confidence in teaching science. For those searching for ideas for fun and practical ways to teach science, this book provides a plethora of ideas that will save the busy teacher time and effort. The fifty activities in this book include the science topics covered, a list of materials needed, vocabulary words linked to the lesson, and literature connections. The literature connections provide examples of children's literature to accompany each activity, a more engaging source for students as compared to the dull narrative typical in science textbooks.

Resources are included for pre-, post-, and during activities, as well as suggestions for teaching vocabulary. Appendixes include activity sheets to accompany specific activities. A "Summary of Activities" section is located at the end of the book that lists the activity title, science topic, vocabulary, and page number for each activity.

CHAPTER CONTENT

Chapter 1 includes activities that connect science and food. Mixing, cooking, and even the use of appliances are connected to physical and chemical sciences.

Chapter 2 describes how to use games to teach science. Games involve rules, interaction, engagement, and competition, as does the scientific method of learning.

Chapter 3 introduces various ways to use literature to teach science. Fiction, nonfiction, poetry, folktales, picture books, novels, and informational books promote self-selected reading and supplement content from science textbooks.

Chapter 4 connects music to science. Early scientists sought to explain how music is an integral part of the universe.

Chapter 5 demonstrates how the community can be used to teach science, including the use of the natural environment. Since science permeates our surroundings, it seems logical to use the natural environment as a learning tool.

Chapter 6 focuses on using everyday objects to teach science. This encourages the use of science to be discovered both at home and in school with very little expense.

The next generation of science students will be responsible for making informed decisions on major issues such as climate change, medical treatments, or use of resources. Interest in or motivation to learn science will affect their future. It is our hope that this book will inspire teachers to create fun and dynamic lessons that encourage student interest in learning and applying science content.

NOTES

1. Materials compiled from Carol Seefeldt, "Teaching Science through the Visual Arts and Music," *Scholastic Early Childhood Today* 18, no. 6 (2004): 29–34; Kim Andrews, *Exploring Nature: Activity Book for Kids* (Emeryville, CA: Rockridge, 2019), 2–3.

2. Karen Worth, "Science in Early Childhood Classrooms: Content and Process," *Early Childhood Research & Practice (ECRP)* 12, no. 2 (2010): 1–17.

3. Steve Spangler, "The Scientific Method," in *10-Minute Science Experiments* (New York: Topix Media Lab, 2019), 14–15.

4. SHARE Team, "Three Ideas for Teaching Science to Elementary Students," *Resilient Educator* (blog), accessed April 11, 2022, https://resilienteducator.com/classroom-resources/3-ideas-for-teaching-science-to-elementary-students/.

5. Yvette F. Greenspan, *A Guide to Teaching Elementary Science: Ten Easy Steps* (Boston: Sense, 2016), 121–23.

6. Greenspan, *Guide to Teaching Elementary Science*, 19–26.

Chapter 1

Using Food to Teach Science

The kitchen is a great place to teach science. Mixing and cooking are closely connected to physical and chemical sciences. Children explore the world by manipulating common objects, including pots and pans, measuring cups, and wooden spoons. Physical and chemical science in elementary school gives students a chance to understand the science of materials they encounter daily.

Begin by sharing the different ways of cooking: roasting, frying, boiling, barbecuing, microwaving, pickling, and smoking. Challenge students to use words to describe characteristics of food: gooey, sticky, puffy, slimy, spicy, tart, salty; or ways to manipulate food: bake, peel, mash, grate, grind, sauté. Using food to teach science allows students to discover food groups, learn how food changes while cooking, explore their five senses, conduct experiments, analyze results, and make predictions.

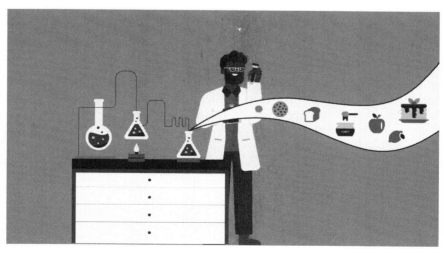

Illustration by Madalyn Stack.

Define food for students as any nutritious substance that people eat or drink in order to stay alive. Talk about how the energy we get from food originates from plants. Discuss with students the compounds we need from food—fats, carbohydrates, proteins, vitamins, minerals, fiber, and water—and why they are important.

Introduce the importance of salt, not only as a flavor enhancer, but also as an essential element for our bodies to use to transmit electric signals through cells to our brains. Salt has been used for preserving food, softening water, preventing ice on roads, and even as a form of currency.[1] Black peppercorns were also used as a form of money and were thought to have curative properties. Ask students to research how salt and pepper became the staple spices for everyday cooking.

There are so many fun ways to integrate food into your science curriculum. Expand your classroom literature to include books about food and favorite recipes of students. Think about which foods can relate to all five senses. For example, when popping popcorn, students can use their senses of smelling, hearing, seeing, tasting, and touching. Start a school or community garden. Prepare recipes in the classroom using hot plates, toasters, or griddles. Invite dietitians or other health experts to speak to students. Plan field trips to local farms, grocery stores, food banks, fisheries, restaurants, or agricultural companies.

The thirteen activities in this chapter explore how students can identify science in their daily intake of food. From grabbing breakfast to an afternoon snack, science is everywhere in the kitchen. Students can explore various types of food as well as how they change during and after cooking. The food in this chapter is full of investigative topics from bubble gum to pancakes. **Please note that not all food in this chapter is fit to eat after the experiments.**

Topics covered in this chapter include: physical and chemical changes in cooking, landfills, oxidation of food, chemistry with carbon dioxide, sense of taste, writing secret messages, types of heat transfer, cloud formation, fossils, iron in food, phases of the moon, changing milk into plastic and glue, and using the scientific method.

ACTIVITIES FOR USING FOOD TO TEACH SCIENCE

1. Pancake Chemistry

Topic: Physical and Chemical Changes with Cooking
Materials Needed: griddle, pancake mix, eggs, milk, spatula, pan, syrup, paper plates, forks, mixing bowl, measuring cups, wooden spoon

Vocabulary:

- Physical change—the form of a substance is changed but not transformed. For example, water freezes, melts, or evaporates, but stays water.
- Chemical change—substances have been combined to change into a new substance
- Gluten—plant proteins found in cereal grains that give cohesiveness to dough

Literature Connections:

Captain Jack. *My Food Comes from the Swamp.* Independently published, 2022.

Carle, Eric. *Pancakes, Pancakes!* Aladdin, 1998.

Debbink, Andrea. *Kitchen Chemistry: A Food Science Cookbook.* American Girl, 2020.

dePaola, Tomie. *Pancakes for Breakfast.* Clarion Books, 2013.

McGinty, Alice B. *Pancakes to Parathas: Breakfast around the World.* Little Bee Books, 2019.

Rey, H. A. *Curious George Makes Pancakes.* Clarion Books, 2019.

Ask students: "How are pancakes connected to science?" Inform students that flour contains *gluten*, which is a protein that provides the chewy texture in pancakes. When moistened, the gluten molecules become active. The more you mix the ingredients, the tighter the bonding of the molecules. When baking powder is added, it creates bubbles in the pancake that the gluten network traps, which allows the pancake to become fluffy.[2]

You can do experiments on the fluffiness of pancakes by making three batches: one mixed until combined but lumpy, one mixed until smooth, and one mixed until smooth and add three to five more minutes of stirring. The first batch allows gluten molecules to remain loose and more bubbles to exist for fluffier pancakes.

The book *Pancakes, Pancakes!* (Carle 1998) presents a pictorial recipe as Jack finds the ingredients for the pancakes: flour from the mill, an egg from the hen, milk from the cow, butter churned from cream, and firewood for the stove. With a small griddle, teachers can cook up pancakes for students to taste. Ask students to decide if they notice a *physical* or *chemical* change when making pancakes.

Use the T-chart in appendix A and have students note the physical and chemical changes when you: measure flour, crack eggs, mix milk, and cook pancakes.[3] Serve up a fresh-made batch of pancakes to the students; then ask: "What kind of change happens when we eat food?"

2. Edible Landfill[4]

Topic: Landfills

Materials Needed: Oreo cookies (4 per student), 8-ounce plastic cups (1 per student), 8-ounce box of raisins, fruit leathers (1 per student), graham crackers (2 per student), red licorice sticks (2 per student), package of birthday candles, box of matches, chocolate ice cream (or pudding) (1 scoop per student), whipped cream (2 tablespoons per student), plastic knives and forks, a variety of small chewable candies (1 handful per student)

Vocabulary:

- Leachate—liquid created when trash decomposes
- Decomposition—decay of a substance
- Methane gas—colorless, odorless gas that is a product of decomposition
- Rodent—small, gnawing animal with sharp front teeth

Literature Connections:

Bradshaw, Erica. *Their Home, Our Landfill.* To Draw Attention, 2018.

French, Jess. *What a Waste: Trash, Recycling, and Protecting Our Planet.* DK Children, 2019.

Heos, Bridget. *Follow That Garbage! A Journey to the Landfill.* Riverstream, 2016.

Winter, Jonah. *Here Comes the Garbage Barge!* Schwartz & Wade, 2010.

Explain to students that a landfill is a large area of land specifically designed to receive wastes. The purpose of a landfill is to eliminate open dumps of the past, which often had harmful and undesirable characteristics that harmed public health and the environment. Landfills have many layers to prevent leakage from the garbage into soil or groundwater. Students will construct their own model landfills in class.

Give each student a cup and four Oreo cookies. Explain that the cup represents an excavated hole in the ground. Have students carefully "unscrew" two of their cookies so that one half has white cream and the other is bare. Encourage students to follow the instructions below:

- Crush the bare cookie halves into small pieces and put them into the cup to represent a layer of soil that is placed in the bottom of real landfills.
- Take the cookie halves with white cream and break them up into two or three pieces. Place the pieces in the cup with the white cream face up, to represent a layer of clay that is put on top of the soil in real landfills.
- Use the plastic knife to cut their fruit leathers to roughly fit the size of the top of the cup and slide the fruit pieces on top of the cookies to represent

a sanitary liner that prevents *leachate* from escaping from a landfill into the ground. The pieces should curl up on the sides of the cup.
- Crush and add the graham crackers to represent a sand layer used to prevent liquids in landfills from seeping out.
- Place raisins on top to represent a layer of pebbles to provide further protection against leachate leaks.
- Rip the licorice sticks in half and bite off both ends to represent leachate pipes that collect any leachate that collects on top of the line. Stick pipes into pebble layer.
- Sprinkle the candies on top of the raisins. The candies represent pieces of garbage.

Ask students: "What happens when a landfill or 'cup' is filled up with trash or 'candies'?" "How can we reduce the amount of trash that we send to the landfill?" Give each student a scoop of ice cream (or pudding) on top of the candies. Then, have the students add one more layer of candies on top of the ice cream. The ice cream layer represents the seepage created from rain seeping through the garbage. Explain that in a real landfill, more layers of garbage are placed on the landfill each day, so that liquid from the *decomposition* of the trash is continually created.

Direct students to "unscrew" their two remaining cookies and crush another layer of the bare cookie halves, without the cream, on top of the candies and ice cream to represent soil again that reduces the amount of rainwater that reaches the garbage. (Students can eat the other cream-covered cookie halves). Each student should use a layer of whipped cream to "cap" the landfill or cover it to prevent odor, insect, and *rodent* problems.

In front of the class, stick a candle (to represent a pipe) deep into your own edible "landfill" and light it to represent the *methane gas* recovery system, which draws methane gas from the decomposing garbage. The flame represents energy that can be generated by burning the captured methane gas. Capturing and burning landfill methane to extract its energy can help reduce greenhouse gas emissions.

Hand out the chart in appendix B; ask students to draw the layers of their landfill and then complete the questions as they eat their landfills as a snack. Remind students that if they built their landfill correctly, their cookies will be dry, just as in a real landfill the soil remains protected from leachate.

3. Brown Apples[5]

Topic: Oxidation
Materials Needed: 1 apple, bottle of lemon juice, glass of water, sharp knife, 3 bowls

Vocabulary:

- Oxidized—combined chemically with oxygen
- Chemical—substance used in or produced by a reaction involving changes to atoms or molecules

Literature Connections:

Priceman, Marjorie. *How to Make an Apple Pie and See the World.* Dragonfly Books, 1996.
Sooy, Julia. *Every Day, Chemistry.* Feiwel & Friends, 2021.
van Hichtum, Nienke. *The Apple Cake.* Floris Books, 2021.

Ask students: "Why do apples turn brown after they are sliced?" Cut the apple into thin slices. Place one slice of apple in each bowl. Cover the second slice with water and the third slice with lemon juice. Leave the bowls for thirty minutes; then check to see which apples turned brown. Explain to students that air contains oxygen, which reacts with *chemicals* in apples to make a brown chemical product. Air has easy access to the cells of the apple when it is by itself.

The apple covered with water goes brown a little slower, as water is in the way. However, water contains dissolved oxygen, which eventually gets into the apple cells. Lemon juice contains vitamin C, which oxygen prefers. Once all the vitamin C gets *oxidized* and used up, the apple will eventually brown. So, the lemon juice will keep the apple fresher for longer. You may have students try other fruits to see which ones go brown first, and try other juices, such as pineapple juice.

4. Pop Rocks and Soda Pop[6]

Topic: Chemistry with Carbon Dioxide
Materials Needed: 4 packets Pop Rocks candy, 4 one-liter bottles of different sodas (e.g., cola, lemon-lime soda, Dr Pepper, root beer) 4 balloons
Vocabulary:

- Hypothesize—give a possible explanation
- Carbon dioxide—colorless, odorless gas formed during respiration

Literature Connections:

Brunelle, Lynn. *Pop Bottle Science.* Workman, 2004.
CQ Products. *Soda Pop Cookbook: 101 Recipes with Soda Pop.* G & R, 2010.
Johnson, J. J. *Iggy & Oz: The Soda Pop Wars.* Dark Side Geeks, 2020.

Pour an entire envelope of Pop Rocks into each balloon. Ask students to *hypothesize* which soda they think will inflate the balloon the biggest or fastest. Remove the lids from the four soda bottles and put the balloons over the openings. Explain that Pop Rocks have *carbon dioxide* bubbles inside that mix with the carbon dioxide in sodas. Because the carbon dioxide has nowhere to go, it rises up and fills the balloon. Repeat the experiment with bottles of water to see what will happen. Have students taste the soda after the experiment. Ask students: "Why does the soda taste flat?" Explain that when soda goes flat, the concentration of carbonic acid in the drink gets lower and the fizz disappears.

5. How Many Ways Do You Taste?[7]

Topic: Sense of Taste
Materials Needed: lemons, cheeses, salted peanuts, candies, coffee, water, sugar, lemon juice, food coloring, spoon, 4 glasses
Vocabulary:

- Salty—seasoned with and tasting of salt
- Bitter—sharp, biting, unpleasant taste
- Sweet—having a taste of sugar or honey
- Savory—delicious and tasty
- Sour—sharp acidic taste, as of vinegar or lemons
- Flavor—distinctive taste of something

Literature Connections:

Boothroyd, Jennifer. *What Is Taste?* Lerner, 2013.
Clark, Bonnie. *Taste Your Words.* WorthyKids, 2020.
Thomas, Sarah. *Kalamata's Kitchen: Taste Buds in Harmony.* Random House Books for Young Readers, 2022.
Tills, Kelly. *Chicks Don't Eat Candy.* FDI, 2022.

Explain to students that the tongue contains taste buds that detect *flavors*. Create sticky notes with the terms *salty*, *bitter*, *sweet*, *savory*, and *sour*. Place on a table all of the food and drink and have students taste the items. Note: Be careful to find out if students are diabetic or have peanut allergies and plan alternative foods to taste. Ask students to place the sticky note that describes the flavor beside the item. If there are disagreements, ask students to justify their choices.

You can actually trick students' taste buds with this experiment. In four glasses, place water, 6 teaspoons sugar, 2 teaspoons lemon juice, and four to six drops food coloring. Put different coloring in each glass (red, blue, yellow, green). Use the chart in appendix C and ask students to taste each drink and mark an X in the box to show what they think is the flavor of each drink. Most times, students will allow their sense of sight to fool them and not realize that all drinks will taste exactly the same. Have students complete the questions with the chart.

6. Secret Food Codes[8]

Topic: Writing Messages with Food
Materials Needed: lemons, honey, water, tonic water, bowls, paintbrushes or cotton swabs, paper, towel, iron, UV flashlight
Vocabulary:

- Organic—being or coming from living plants and animals
- Dilute—make a liquid weaker or thinner
- Consensus—general agreement among a group of people

Literature Connections:

Caswell, Deanna. *Making Secret Codes and Messages*. Black Rabbit Books, 2018.
Javaherbin, Mina. *The Secret Message*. Hyperion Book CH, 2010.
Roman, Carole P. *Spies, Code Breakers, and Secret Agents: A World War II Book for Kids*. Rockridge, 2020.

Tell students that they can use food to write secret messages. Divide students into three groups. For group 1, squeeze lemon juice into the bowls and have students use the paintbrushes or cotton swabs and juice to write their messages on paper. Allow the paper to dry. Place the paper over a towel and carefully apply heat from an iron until the message appears.

Ask students: "Why does the message appear when heated?" (the *organic* substances in lemons break down and turn brown). For group 2, *dilute* honey with water and have students paint a message. Use the towel and iron to reveal the message. Ask the same question to students in this group: "Why does the message appear when heated?" (when honey caramelizes, it turns brown). For group 3, place tonic water in the bowls and have students paint a message. Shine the UV flashlight on the message and it will appear. Turn off the flashlight and the message will disappear. Ask students to come to a *consensus* on the best way to write secret messages and why.

7. Don't Burn the Toast

Topic: Types of Heat Transfer
Materials Needed: hot plate, toaster, griddle, various foods to cook

Vocabulary:

- Conduction—heat transferred between objects through direct contact
- Convection—combines conduction heat transfer and circulation to force molecules in the air to move from warmer areas to cooler ones
- Radiation—heat and light waves strike and penetrate food

Literature Connections:

Binczewski, Kim. *Bread Lab!* Readers to Eaters, 2022.
Dooley, Norah. *Everybody Bakes Bread.* First Avenue Editions, 1995.
Kleven, Elisa. *Sun Bread.* Puffin Books, 2004.
Maillard, Kevin Noble. *Fry Bread: A Native American Family Story.* Roaring Brook, 2019.
Maurer, Daniel D. *Do You Really Want to Burn Your Toast? A Book about Heat.* Riverstream, 2016.
Morris, Ann. *Bread, Bread, Bread (Foods of the World).* HarperCollins, 1993.

Introduce students to the three types of heat transfer: *conduction*, *convection*, and *radiation*. Share the book *Do You Really Want to Burn Your Toast? A Book about Heat* (Maurer 2016) with students and discuss how heat and energy can be used to cook food. In the book, two children make their parents breakfast, investigate how metal is a conductor of heat, and learn about reactions that are reversible and those that are not.

Use a hot plate, toaster, or griddle in the classroom to cook food with students. Ask students to determine what type of heat transfer is used. Share different ways that bread is cooked around the world and methods used to cook the bread. Have a bread-tasting day!

8. Mostly Cloudy[9]

Topic: Types of Clouds
Materials Needed: glass jar with lid, boiling water, hair spray, ice cubes, measuring cup, hair conditioner, cornstarch, cotton candy flavor (or any blue) gelatin, whipped cream, vanilla ice cream, lemon-lime soda, blue food coloring, clear glasses and bowls, spoons, parchment paper, Ivory soap, wax paper
Vocabulary:

- Cirrus—thin, wispy clouds at high altitudes that may contain ice crystals
- Cumulus—dense, white, fluffy clouds associated with fair weather
- Stratus—low, flat, gray clouds
- Nimbus—large gray clouds that bring rain or snow

Literature Connections:

dePaola, Tomie. *The Cloud Book*. Holiday House, 1975.

Fan, Terry. *Lizzy and the Cloud*. Simon & Schuster Books for Young Readers, 2022.

Hodgson, Rob. *When Cloud Became a Cloud*. Rise x Penguin Workshop, 2021.

Kooser, Ted. *Marshmallow Clouds: Two Poets at Play among Figures of Speech*. Candlewick, 2022.

Discuss with students how clouds consist of billions of tiny droplets of water. The water droplets condense around small pieces of dust or other pollutants. Show students pictures of types of clouds: *cirrus, cumulus, stratus, nimbus*. Have students research questions about clouds: "Why do clouds float?" "Why are clouds white?" "How do clouds move?"

Boil ⅓ cup water and pour it into the jar. Quickly spray the hair spray into the jar to give the water vapor a surface to condense into cloud droplets. Screw on the lid and place ice cubes on top; then watch the cloud form (or place the lid upside down to cover the opening completely and place the ice cubes in the lid). Some experiments use a lit match to drop into the jar to form condensation. Remind students that a cloud needs water vapor, a pollutant, and a change in air temperature and pressure to form.

Use 1 cup hair conditioner and 2 cups cornstarch to make cloud dough. You can use food coloring or glitter to spice up your clouds. Parchment paper is a must as a place to model clouds, and airtight containers can preserve the dough.

Cloud desserts can top off the day. Follow the directions to mix the blue gelatin and let it set in a refrigerator for several hours. Cut into sections and layer in a glass bowl with whipped cream. Dye lemon-lime soda blue with food coloring (about five drops). Scoop vanilla ice cream into clear glasses and pour over the blue soda. Both desserts display the blue sky intermixed with white clouds.

The teacher can demonstrate how to make a cloud by microwaving a bar of white Ivory soap. Place the soap on a sheet of wax paper and microwave for ninety seconds. Be careful because the cloud will be hot. Shape the fluffy ball into cloud formations.

9. Baking Footprints[10]

Topic: Fossils

Materials Needed: baking sheet, aluminum foil, 2 mixing bowls, measuring cups, 1¼ cups all-purpose flour, ½ teaspoon baking soda, ¼ teaspoon

baking powder, ⅓ cup butter (softened), ⅔ cup granulated sugar, 1 tablespoon powdered sugar, 1 egg, ½ teaspoon vanilla extract, items for creating fossil imprints (e.g., leaves, shells, plastic bugs or dinosaurs)
Vocabulary:

- Paleontologist—scientist who studies fossils
- Fossil—impression of an animal or plant that has been preserved in rock

Literature Connections:

Becker, Helaine. *The Fossil Whisperer: How Wendy Sloboda Discovered a Dinosaur.* Kids Can, 2022.
Diehn, Andi. *Fossil Huntress: Mary Leakey, Paleontologist.* Nomad, 2019.
Laverdunt, Damien, and Helene Rajcak. *Fossils from Lost Worlds.* Gecko, 2021.
Thomson, Bill. *Fossil.* Two Lions, 2013.

Discuss with students how *paleontologists* learn information about extinct plants or animals through the study of *fossils*. Ask students to brainstorm what they think we can learn from fossils (e.g., what an animal ate, how it walked, where it lived, how it died). Ask students: "Where are fossils found?" (riverbeds, lakes, caves, tar pits, volcanic ash falls).

Line baking sheet with aluminum foil. Mix together flour, baking soda, and baking powder and set aside. In another bowl, mix butter and both sugars. Beat in the egg and vanilla. Slowly add the dry ingredients to the wet ingredients and continue to mix. Roll the dough into tablespoon-size balls and place on the baking sheet about two inches apart. Dip the items for creating fossil imprints into flour; then push into each ball. (Note: Do not leave items used for imprints in the dough during baking.) Bake for eight minutes in a 375-degree preheated oven. Let cool; then enjoy!

10. Iron for Breakfast[11]

Topic: Iron in Food
Materials Needed: Total cereal, strong magnet, plastic zip bag, water, ½ cup measuring cup
Vocabulary:

- Dissolve—to be absorbed by a liquid when mixed
- Soluble—able to be dissolved in liquid
- Fortify—add nutrients to food

Literature Connections:

Fisher, Valorie. *Now You Know What You Eat*. Orchard Books, 2019.
Hawkins, Linda J. *Alexander and the Great Food Fight*. Heart to Heart, 2005.
Kurlansky, Mark. *The Story of Salt*. Puffin Books, 2014.
Mooney, Carla. *The Chemistry of Food*. Nomad, 2021.
Rockwell, Lizzy. *Good Enough to Eat: A Kid's Guide to Food and Nutrition*. HarperCollins, 2009.

Inform students that iron is an essential mineral to keep the body's cells, skin, hair, and nails healthy. It is the substance in red blood cells that carries oxygen throughout the body. Iron is naturally present in many foods: beef, pork, turkey, raisins, spinach, walnuts, cashews, peanuts. Since the 1940s, food manufacturers have *fortified* cereal with vitamins and minerals. Without fortification, most cereals have little nutritional value. Try this experiment with students to find iron in cereal.

Encourage students to pour out some cereal and try to attract the iron using a magnet. Ask students: "Why doesn't the cereal attract to the magnet?" Pour ½ cup cereal into the plastic zip bag (it helps if you crush the cereal into a powder). Fill half the bag with water and let the water and cereal mixture sit for one hour. Place the magnet in your hand; then place the bag on top. Swish around for fifteen to twenty seconds; then flip the bag over so that the magnet is on top. Examine the collection of iron and move it around with the magnet.

Try the experiment with other cereals to see if the results are the same. Ask students to determine which cereals are more *soluble*. Explain that when cereal *dissolves* in water, the iron does not dissolve. The iron added to cereal is just like the iron that goes into metal nails and is strongly attracted to magnets.

11. Eating the Moon

Topic: Phases of the Moon
Materials Needed: can of white icing, large round cookies, plastic knives, pencil and Styrofoam ball for each student, lamp
Vocabulary:

- Phase—any of the forms in which the moon appears
- Gibbous—more than half full
- Waxing—gradual increase
- Waning—gradual decrease

- Crescent—arc shape in first and last quarters of the moon
- Counterclockwise—in the opposite direction to the way in which clock hands move
- Illuminate—brighten with light

Literature Connections:

Canavan, Thomas. *What Does the Moon Taste Like?* Arcturus, 2020.
Courgeon, Remi. *Many Moons.* Walter Foster Jr., 2017.
Grejniec, Michael. *A Taste of the Moon.* Bright Connections Media, 2013.
Milbourne, Anna. *On the Moon.* Usborne, 2006.
Teckentrup, Britta. *Moon: A Peek-Through Picture Book.* Doubleday Books for Young Readers, 2018.

Pose the question to students: "Why does the moon look different shapes at night?" Explain that as the moon orbits around the earth, the amount of sunlight reflected off the moon controls how much of the moon we see. Show students pictures of the *phases* of the moon—new, *waxing crescent*, first quarter, *waxing gibbous*, full, *waning gibbous*, last quarter, *waning crescent*—at the NASA Science website (https://moon.nasa.gov/moon-in-motion /moon-phases/).

Place a lamp (representing the sun) in the middle of the room without the lampshade. Use at least a 100-watt bulb. Have students poke their pencils into the Styrofoam balls (representing the moon) and hold them out in front of their bodies at shoulder length. Students are representing the earth and will rotate where they are around the sun (lamp).

To show new moon, have students face the sun and hold their moon directly in front of them to explain that from the earth the new moon is not seen. To show waxing crescent, have students turn their bodies forty-five degrees *counterclockwise* to see the right-hand side of their moon *illuminated*. To show first quarter, have students continue turning left so that they are ninety degrees from their original position.

As students continue to turn, they will see more and more illuminated surface on their moon. When students' backs are to the sun, have them hold up their moon so that the light is not blocked to see the full moon. As students continue to turn, have them identify waning gibbous, last quarter, and waning crescent.[12]

Provide students with plastic knives and have them create the moon phases by using icing on each cookie. Place the cookie moon phases in a circle in order of the phases. Teach the following poem to students before allowing them to eat the cookies:

The moon is a cookie, big and round
That crosses the sky without a sound
And slowly disappears around
With nary a crumb that can be found

12. Milky Magic[13]

Topic: Chemical Changes with Milk
Materials Needed: milk, small pot, spoon, vinegar, strainer, jar, paper tow-
els, measuring cup, tablespoon, baking soda
Vocabulary:

• Casein—comprises about 80 percent of the proteins in cow's milk; used
in processed foods, adhesives, paints, and other industrial products

Literature Connections:

Coelho, Alexa. *Why is Milk White? & 200 Other Curious Chemistry
Questions.* Chicago Review, 2013.
French, Vivian. *Oliver's Milk Shake.* Orchard, 2001.
Gibbons, Gail. *The Milk Makers.* Aladdin, 1987.
Heos, Bridget. *From Milk to Cheese (Who Made My Lunch?).* Amicus
Ink, 2018.
Herrington, Lisa M. *Milk to Ice Cream (Rookie Read-About Science: How
Things Are Made).* Children's Press, 2013.

Milk can be transformed into a malleable plastic molding material with
just a few ingredients. Pour 1 cup milk into a pot to warm, but not boil. Add
a tablespoon of vinegar and stir for about three minutes. Place the strainer
on top of the jar and pour the mixture through the strainer. Place the remaining material on a paper towel and blot off the moisture. The solid material
is called *casein* and is used by industries to make glue, plastics, and paints.
Mold the casein (or make impressions in the plastic) and allow to dry for one
to two days. The casein can be used for a variety of projects, such as a button
replacement, guitar pick, toy wheel, or bottle cap.

Inquire of students: "Is this a physical or chemical reaction?" (This is a
chemical reaction. The protein casein breaks apart when milk is heated above
80 degrees Celsius and the pH is lowered below 4.5 with the vinegar. Milk
converts into curd, which is a new substance, and the process is irreversible.)

To change milk into glue, follow the same process to make the casein.
Place the casein back in the pot on the stove and add ¼ cup water and a tablespoon of baking soda. The casein material will begin to bubble, and when it
stops, the leftover material can be used as glue. Be sure to wait several hours
for the glue to dry.

13. Scientific Bubble Gum[14]

Topic: Using the Scientific Method

Materials Needed: bubble gum for each pair of students (2 different brands labeled A and B), recording sheet, ruler, 12-inch piece of string, 2 small pieces of wax paper

Vocabulary:

- Scientific method—the process of asking questions, observing, and seeking answers through tests and experiments. The five steps include:
  - Identify a problem—develop a question that can be answered through observation
  - Observe/research—gather information before the experiment using five senses
  - Make a hypothesis/prediction—make an educated guess of the outcome based on information already known
  - Experiment—conduct an experiment to test the hypothesis
  - Analyze data/draw conclusions—look at the results of the experiment to determine if the hypothesis is supported

Literature Connections:

Allegra, Mike. *Scamper Thinks Like a Scientist*. Dawn, 2019.
Kramer, Stephen P. *How to Think Like a Scientist: Answering Questions by the Scientific Method*. HarperCollins, 1987.
O'Brien, Jim. *The Bubble Gum Girl*. Lanier, 2016.
Wheeler, Lisa. *Bubble Gum, Bubble Gum*. Purple House, 2019.

Introduce or review the steps of the *scientific method*. Show students the two brands of bubble gum and introduce the problem: "Which bubble gum brand blows the biggest bubble?" Using the chart in appendix D, have students make three observations about each type of bubble gum, such as, How does it smell? Is it sugar-free or full of sugar? What is the size of the gum? Ask students to write their hypothesis to predict which brand will blow the biggest bubble and why.

Divide students into pairs and assign one to chew brand A bubble gum, and one to chew brand B. The student with brand A should chew their gum for three minutes and then blow a bubble. The partner will measure the diameter across the bubble with the string, then lay the string on the ruler to measure the number of centimeters. Repeat the process to blow two more bubbles and record the data on the table. Add all the diameters and divide by 3 to get the average bubble size for brand A. The student with brand B should repeat the process. Have the partners write a conclusion on which brand of gum is the best at blowing bubbles and why. Other experiments can include which gum flavor lasts longer or how stretching ability, hardness, or sugar content affects bubble size.

MORE FOOD AND LITERATURE CONNECTIONS:

Barrett, Judi. *Cloudy with a Chance of Meatballs.* Atheneum Books for Young Readers, 1982.
Bingham, Winsome. *Soul Food Sunday.* Harry N. Abrams, 2021.
dePaola, Tomie. *Strega Nona.* Simon & Schuster Books for Young Readers, 1979.
Ehlert, Lois. *Eating the Alphabet.* HMH Books for Young Readers, 1996.
Gates, Stefan. *Science You Can Eat.* DK, 2019.
Gilmore, Lorena K. Lazo. *Cora Cooks Pancit.* Lee & Low Books, 2014.
Green, Rebecca. *My Perfect Cupcake: A Recipe for Thriving with Food Allergies.* Tabby Cat, 2021.
Iwai, Melissa. *Dumplings for Lili.* Norton Young Readers, 2021.
Jalapeno, Jake. *The Silly Food Book.* Independently published, 2021.
Lakshmi, Padma. *Tomatoes for Neela.* Viking Books for Young Readers, 2021.
Larios, Julie. *Delicious! Poems Celebrating Street Food around the World.* Beach Lane Books, 2021.
Lauber, Patricia. *Who Eats What? Food Chains and Food Webs.* HarperCollins, 2016.
Liguore, Hunter. *The Whole World inside Nan's Soup.* Yeehoo, 2021.
Lopez-Alt, J. Kenji. *Every Night Is Pizza Night.* Norton Young Readers, 2020.
Northness, Cheryl. *Petey Pete and the Food Fairy: A Food Rescue Story.* Isabella Machelle, 2021.
O'Neill, Diane. *Saturday at the Food Pantry.* Albert Whitman, 2021.
Penfold, Alexandra. *Food Truck Fest!* Farrar, Straus and Giroux (BYR), 2018.
Rubin, Adam. *Dragons Love Tacos.* Scholastic, 2013.
Seuss, Dr. *Green Eggs and Ham.* Random House, 1960.
Sharmat, Mitchell. *Gregory, the Terrible Eater.* Scholastic, 2009.
Soto, Gary. *Too Many Tamales.* Puffin Books, 1996.
Stanley, Diane. *Alice Waters Cooks Up a Food Revolution.* Simon & Schuster/Paula Wiseman Books, 2022.
Vardell, Sylvia, and Janet Wong. *Things We Eat.* Pomelo Books, 2022.

NOTES

1. Stefan Gates, *Science You Can Eat* (New York: DK, 2019), 20–21.

2. Adapted from lesson "The Scientific Secret of Fluffy Pancakes," by Esme Trontz, *CityScience* (blog), *Scientific American*, September 12, 2013, https://www.scientificamerican.com/article/bring-science-home-gluten-pancakes/.

3. Adapted from lesson "Kitchen Chemistry," by Christine Anne Royce, Emily Morgan, and Karen Ansberry, *Teaching Science through Trade Books* (Arlington, VA: National Science Teachers Association, 2012), 127–30.

4. Adapted from lesson "Luscious Layered Landfill," by Environmental Protection Agency (EPA), *A Teacher's Guide to Reducing, Reusing, and Recycling: The Quest for Less (Activities and Resources for Teaching K–8)* (Washington, DC: Environmental Protection Agency, 2005), 173–75.

5. Adapted from lesson "How to Keep Fruit from Going Brown," *Kitchen Chemistry Experiments* (blog), *Fizzics Education*, accessed March 10, 2022, https://www.fizzicseducation.com.au/150-science-experiments/kitchen-chemistry-experiments/how-to-keep-fruit-from-going-brown-2/.

6. Adapted from lesson "Pop Rock Science Experiment for Kids," by Beth Gorden, *123Homeschool4ME* (blog), accessed March 2, 2021, https://www.123homeschool4me.com/pop-rock-science-experiment-for-kids_70/.

7. Gates, *Science You Can Eat*, 10–13.

8. Gates, *Science You Can Eat*, 56–57.

9. Adapted from lesson "Clouds Science for Kids: 23 Smart Ideas for the Classroom," *Teach Junkie* (blog), accessed April 13, 2022, https://www.teachjunkie.com/sciences/clouds-science-for-kids/.

10. Adapted from lesson "Bake Your Own Fossils," by Kim Andrews, *Exploring Nature: Activity Book for Kids* (Emeryville, CA: Rockridge, 2019), 64–65.

11. Adapted from lesson "Iron for Breakfast," by Steve Spangler, *10-Minute Science Experiments* (New York: Topix Media Lab, 2019), 154–57.

12. Adapted from lesson "Moon Phases," by NASA, Jet Propulsion Laboratory: California Institute of Technology, accessed March 20, 2022, https://www.jpl.nasa.gov/edu/teach/activity/moon-phases/.

13. Adapted from lessons "Got Plastic? Turn Milk into Sneaky Plastic" and "Need Glue? Create Sneaky Glue from Milk," by Cy Tymony, *Sneaky Uses for Everyday Things* (Kansas City, MO: Andrews McMeel, 2020), 8–12.

14. Adapted from lesson "Scientific Method Lab Using Bubble Gum," by Brad Bauer from Minnesota Science Teachers Education Project, Hamline University Graduate School of Education, accessed October 10, 2022, https://serc.carleton.edu/sp/mnstep/activities/27600.html.

Chapter 2

Using Games to Teach Science

Children typically play sports-related games, or make up games that mimic real life. Games involve rules, interaction, engagement, and competition, as often does the scientific method of learning. Games encourage creative expression and allow for varied learning styles. By playing games, students have opportunities to make decisions and solve problems. Often, games are played spontaneously for fun and enjoyment. There does not always have to be losers in games—students can obtain success without others failing.[1]

Most any game can be modified for a science class. Some examples are listed below:

- Science baseball revolves around asking students science questions and keeping score. Players who miss the answer get a strike against the team. Players who answer a question correctly get to advance to a base.

Illustration by Madalyn Stack.

Questions should get progressively more difficult. Play nine innings (rounds), and the highest-scoring team wins.

- Going on a nature walk allows the teacher to play "I spy" with students. You can teach students names of plants ("I spy with my little eye a daffodil"), animals ("I spy with my little eye a sparrow"), measurements ("I spy with my little eye something one inch tall"), or even cloud formations ("I spy with my little eye a cumulus cloud shaped like a rabbit"). Challenge students to make their own clues and see who can make the best clue.
- With charades, students can work as teams to act out a word ("biology") or phrase ("theory of relativity") and have the other teams guess the answer. The team that guesses correctly gets to act out the next word or phrase.
- Bingo can be used as a science vocabulary review. Give each student a blank bingo card from the "Vocabulary Activities" in the "Resources" section of this book and have them write in the boxes some of the science words from the unit of study, or just science words they know. Read the definitions and have students place an X on the word on their card that matches. (You might ask students to tell you the word aloud as a check.) The student with the most Xs wins the game.

In today's world, students are connected to constantly evolving technology through personal computers, gaming systems, smartphones, and smart televisions. With the mandate of the job market of future workers to have technology skills, teachers are responsible to integrate forms of technology into the curriculum to help students develop those skills. With access to exceptional websites such as BrainPOP and Discovery Education, students can learn specific science content through animated videos, visuals, interactive activities, and problems to solve.[2]

Computer games and simulations have the capacity to advance the learning of science skills and processes and allow students to interact with representations of natural processes, engage in learning catered to individual styles, and gain immediate feedback. The rapid advancements in hardware and software have increased the reality of the experiences. Students can play on laptops, video consoles, or even their phones. With augmented reality (AR) games, students can step into a virtual world and solve complex problems. Computer simulations and games support a model of inquiry-based learning that overcomes logistical constraints.[3]

The activities in this chapter get students up and moving their bodies and brains. Have you ever wondered why bird beaks are all different, or what kind of rock that is in your backyard? This chapter will answer those questions as well as how to foster a love for science for students of all ages. The eight activities in chapter 2 include ways to use games to teach science. Topics covered include: famous scientists; characteristics of earth; adaptations of bird beaks, animals, and worms; habitats; types of rocks; and learning science through video games.

ACTIVITIES FOR USING GAMES TO TEACH SCIENCE

14. Guess the Scientist

Topic: Famous Scientists
Materials Needed: note cards to write facts, research materials
Vocabulary:

- Nobel Prize—international prize awarded annually for outstanding work in physics, chemistry, physiology or medicine, literature, economics, and the promotion of peace
- Obscure—not known to many people

Literature Connections:

Biskup, Agnieszka, and Sonia Leong. *Marie Curie: A Graphic History of the World's Most Famous Female Scientist (Great Lives).* B.E.S., 2019.

Ferrie, Chris. *Scientist, Scientist, Who Do You See? A Rhyming Book about Famous Scientists for Kids.* Sourcebooks Explore, 2020.

Fortey, Jacqueline. *DK Eyewitness Books: Great Scientists: Discover the Pioneers Who Changed the Way We Think about Our World.* DK Children, 2007.

McKissack, Patricia, and Fredrick McKissack. *George Washington Carver: Scientist and Inventor (Famous African Americans).* Enslow, 2013.

Sis, Peter. *Starry Messenger: A Book Depicting the Life of a Famous Scientist, Mathematician, Astronomer, Philosopher, Physicist, Galileo Galilei.* San Val, 2000.

Washington, Danni. *Bold Women in Science: 15 Women in History You Should Know (Biographies for Kids).* Rockridge, 2021.

Divide students into teams of two to three people. Have each team research a scientist and find five to ten interesting facts. Arrange the facts in order from the least known to the best known fact about the scientist. Give students the organizing directions for creating the clues:

Write the clues in first person (I am . . . , I wrote . . . , I was . . .). Students may want to start with *obscure* facts. Present them in reverse from most difficult to least difficult (for scoring purposes). Some ideas for clues include:

- Little-known or obscure fact
- Hint as to the scientist
- Birthplace and/or family information
- More hints as to the scientist
- Most famous scientific discovery/theory/and so forth

End with "I am . . . ?" before revealing your scientist's name

Students use the clues to identify the scientist. Make the statements, one at a time, giving the other team(s) a chance to guess. The team identifying the correct scientist with the fewest clues receives the most points. The team with the most points at the end of the game wins. Below is an example of clues:

- I was born in Poland but later moved to Paris.
- I often fainted from hunger because I had little money.
- I designed mobile X-ray machines to aid field hospitals in World War I.
- I won *Nobel Prizes* in both physics and chemistry.
- I was the first woman in history to be awarded the Nobel Prize.
- I came up with the word "radioactivity."
- I am . . . Marie Curie.

15. Toss the Globe

Topic: Characteristics of Earth
Materials Needed: inflatable globe
Vocabulary:

- Globe—spherical representation of the earth
- Characteristic—distinguishing quality or feature

Literature Connections:

Cosneau, Geraldine. *All around the World: Animal Kingdom.* Tate, 2011.
Evans, Tom, and Paul Kobasa. *Plants around the World.* World Book, 2011.
Hyde, Natalie. *Earth's Landforms and Bodies of Water (Earth's Processes Close-Up).* Crabtree, 2015.
Kalman, Bobbie. *What Is Climate? (Big Science Ideas).* Crabtree, 2012.

Use an inflatable *globe* to teach communication skills to peers. In pairs, the students pass the globe back and forth as they ask questions, make statements, and give information based on where their right thumb lands. The person catching the globe will answer a science question, such as: What plant/flower grows well in the area near your right thumb? What animals can be found in the country near your right thumb? Describe the physical *characteristics* and names of countries in the continent near your right thumb. Name the lakes and oceans in the continent near your right thumb. What mountain range is closest to your thumb's location? Easy questions are asked first with more thoughtful ones following, such as: Identify the climate in the region near your right thumb. Where is the nearest fault line? What volcanic activity might happen near your thumb?

16. Bird Beaks[4]

Topic: Animal Adaptations
Materials Needed: "bird food" (rice, macaroni, beans, cooked spaghetti, gummy worms, raisins, birdseed, bowl of water), "bird beaks" (toothpicks, clothespins, chopsticks, spoons, small fishing nets), paper cup for each student
Vocabulary:

• Adaptation—the process by which a species becomes better able to survive in its habitat

Literature Connections:

Levine, Sara. *A Peek at Beaks: Tools Birds Use*. Millbrook, 2021.
Page, Robin. *The Beak Book*. Beach Lane Books, 2021.
Sibley, David Allen. *What It's Like to Be a Bird: From Flying to Nesting, Eating to Singing—What Birds Are Doing, and Why*. Knopf, 2020.
Thompson, Mya. *Ruby's Birds*. Cornell Lab, 2020.

Show pictures of various types of birds and have students note what is similar and what is different among them. Point out that birds have different types of beaks to help them get food and survive. Compare beaks to tools: jackhammer, tweezers, nutcracker. Place the "bird food" on a table. Give each student one "bird beak" to use to get food. To play the game, give students one minute to get as much food as they can put in their paper cups.

Have students explain how their beak was significant in catching their food. Discuss how this is relevant to birds and how different *adaptations* allow each type of beak to catch a certain food. Ask students to use the Bird Beaks Investigation Log in appendix E to conduct further experiments with bird beaks.

Share the information below about bird beaks and have students find pictures of birds with these types of beaks:

• Cracker—seed eaters like sparrows and cardinals; short, thick, conical bill
• Shredder—birds of prey like hawks and owls; sharp, curved bills for tearing meat

- Chisel—woodpeckers; bills that are long and chisel-like for boring into wood
- Probe—hummingbirds; long and slender for probing flowers for nectar
- Strainer—ducks; long, flat bills that strain small plants and animals from water

17. Catch Me If You Can[5]

Topic: Habitats

Materials Needed: 6 cardboard boxes to represent bushes; 2 rugs to represent rabbit and fox sleeping areas; blue craft paper cut to represent stream; blue craft paper cut to represent puddle; copies of animal tracks (red fox, cottontail rabbit, gray squirrel); images of the animals; images of food, water, and shelter resources; 5x7 index cards to paste images; 3 food stickers, 1 water sticker, and 1 shelter sticker for each animal (one set per student) and bags to hold the stickers

Vocabulary:

- Habitat—the type of environment in which an organism lives
- Organism—a living thing that can act or function independently
- Terrain—a piece of ground having specific characteristics

Literature Connections:

Jenkins, Steve. *I See a Kookaburra! Discovering Animal Habitats around the World*. HMH Books for Young Readers, 2016.
Kieber-King, Cynthia. *Habitat Spy*. Arbordale, 2015.
Murray, Lily. *Hidden Habitats: Water*. Big Press, 2021.
Piketty, Lucile. *Whose Habitat Is That?* Wide Eyed Editions, 2020.

Set up the area for the game with the bush boxes, rugs, and blue craft paper. Place a box of stickers by each area for students to get and place on their cards. Divide the students into three groups (fox, rabbit, squirrel), and give them the 5x7 index cards with a picture of their animal and the footprint pasted onto the cards. Tape animal tracks on the floor around the room, keeping in mind that foxes have larger ranges than rabbits.

Encourage students to use the sound and movement of their animal as they follow the tracks. On the back of the index cards, have symbols for food, water, and shelter. Students must place the appropriate stickers they find for their animal by the symbols (3 food, 1 water, 1 shelter). Allow one fox, one rabbit, and one squirrel to go at a time; wait a few seconds, then send the next group. Students should collect all the stickers for their animal by carefully following the tracks of their animal and by respecting others as they move about the game area.

Have students rest in the shelter areas, and pretend to drink water and eat food to survive. Debrief the game by having students articulate where the animals slept, what they ate, and where they found water to drink. Have students apply the vocabulary words to the activity.

18. Rock Scavenger Hunt with GPS

Topic: Types of Rocks
Materials Needed: containers, rocks, clipboards, GPS units
Vocabulary:

• Sedimentary—type of rock formed by fragments of other rocks
• Metamorphic—rock formed into a new type of rock through pressure, heat, and time
• Igneous—rock formed when molten magma (from a volcano) cools

Literature Connections:

Jansen, Carla Mae. *A Dinosaur Made Me Sneeze: A Rock Cycle Adventure.* Turtle Trails, 2021.
Miller, Pat Zietlow. *What Can You Do with a Rock?* Sourcebooks Jabberwocky, 2021.
Mr. Jay. *Ricky, the Rock That Couldn't Roll.* New Paige, 2021.
Rosinsky, Natalie Myra. *Rocks: Hard, Soft, Smooth, and Rough.* Picture Window Books, 2002.

Technology can be infused into a scavenger hunt game by using GPS units. Place a number of hidden containers (caches) on the school grounds. Place a different type of rock in each cache. Give groups of students a GPS unit, coordinates to each cache, and a clipboard on which to take notes. As each cache is found, have students identify the type of rock (*sedimentary*, *metamorphic*, or *igneous*), draw a picture of the rock, describe characteristics of the rock, and give a practical use for the rock.

A variation of the game would be to have students go to several coordinates that have lots of rocks. Next, ask students to find rocks that have two colors, are as small as a fingernail, are shaped like an object, and so on.

19. Birds and Worms[6]

Topic: Animal Adaptations
Materials Needed: equal numbers of small pieces of yarn in at least 3 different colors for each member of the class

Vocabulary:

- Camouflage—disguise to help blend in or appear hidden
- Adaptation—a change in a trait that helps an organism survive
- Habitat—place that contains the resources an animal needs to survive

Literature Connections:

Cronin, Doreen. *Diary of a Worm.* Scholastic, 2004.
Dewey, Jennifer. *Can You Find Me? A Book about Animal Camouflage.* Scholastic, 1989.
Jenkins, Steve, and Robin Page. *Look Again: Secrets of Animal Camouflage.* Clarion Books, 2019.
Tildes, Phyllis Limbacher. *Animals in Camouflage.* Charlesbridge, 2000.

Ask students: "What is *camouflage*?" "Which animals do you know that have camouflage?" Tell students that some animals change their fur or feathers from brown in summer to white in winter (e.g., snowshoe hare and ptarmigan). This is known as an *adaptation.* Some animals have a two-toned appearance to blend in with their surroundings. Both prey and predators often have adapted to blend in with the environment or *habitat.*

Prepare the same number and colors of yarn for each student. It works best if at least one of the colors stands out in the designated area and at least one blends in to the colors of the area. For example, in a patch of grass, green and brown tend to blend, but red and yellow stick out. Decide on a designated space for the activity to take place outdoors. Clearly define the boundaries and then randomly place all the pieces of yarn in the area.

Divide students into groups of four or five members. Inform students that they are going to pretend to be hungry birds hunting for worms. Host a relay race in which one student from each team will "fly" (walk around with arms out like wings) over the area and pick up the first worm they see. After one team member gets their worm, they will go to the back of the line and sit down. The next student in line will fly off to hunt. The first team to get all their birds back with a worm wins bragging rights.

Once all teams have finished, allow students to do a second round of hunting for worms. When all teams have finished, use the Birds and Worms Recording Log in appendix F and have each student write down the colors of each of their worms, making sure to indicate which came from round 1 and which from round 2. Before leaving the area, either reset the simulation for the next class (if you teach the same subject to multiple groups of students) or clean up all materials. Make it a game to see who has the best "eagle eyes" and can find the most pieces of yarn.

When back in the classroom, make a tally chart recording the number of each color worm found by the class for round 1 and round 2. Ask students: "Which color worm was easiest to find?" "Which color worm was the hardest to find? Why?" "Which color worm would you want to be?" "What patterns do you see from the class data?" The key concept for this activity is adaptation. The color of the worm was an adaptation that allowed it to survive.

Introduce the vocabulary word "camouflage" to explain how physical characteristics of animals help them survive in their habitat. Ask students to think about what would happen if the same "worms" (pieces of yarn) were moved to a different environment. Challenge them to think of a location where the red and yellow would have an advantage over the brown and green. Extend their learning by having students take the data from the tally chart to create a graph.

20. Pipe Cleaner Camouflage[7]

Topic: Animal Adaptations
Materials Needed: pictures of different biome habitats, pipe cleaners (variety of colors), papers of different colors and patterns (e.g., scrapbook paper, magazine pages)
Vocabulary:

- Adaptation—a change in a trait that helps an organism survive
- Biome—major ecological community type area classified according to the species that live in that location (e.g., tropical rain forest, grassland, desert, tundra)
- Camouflage—disguise to help blend in or appear hidden
- Habitat—place that contains the resources an animal needs to survive
- Mimicry—the close external resemblance of an animal or plant (or part of one) to another animal, plant, or inanimate object

Literature Connections:

Dewey, Jennifer. *Can You Find Me? A Book about Animal Camouflage.* Scholastic, 1989.
Jenkins, Steve, and Robin Page. *Look Again: Secrets of Animal Camouflage.* Clarion Books, 2019.
Tildes, Phyllis Limbacher. *Animals in Camouflage.* Charlesbridge, 2000.

Have pictures of different *biome habitats* on the board. Ask students to name animals that live in each of the biomes. Lead a discussion about similarities between each of the animals in the biome. Ask students: "How do the coverings of animals help them survive in their environment?" Introduce the idea that by having colors similar to their environment, animals are *camouflaged*. Predators cannot tell the prey from their surroundings. Introduce the vocabulary terms and use the literature connections to show examples of animals that use camouflage and *mimicry*. For older students, address different types of mimicry: Batesian, automimicry, aggressive mimicry, and Mullerian.

Challenge students to create a new creature by applying the techniques of camouflage to help their creature survive. Provide students with a choice of pipe cleaners laid out on a table. Either provide students with a variety of background papers on the table or allow them to use a specific area in the school as their biome. Students would need to select a specific spot in the area to be their creature's habitat. Remind students that they can implement color and texture to help their creature camouflage (*adaptation*). They can also use mimicry to look like something that already exists in the habitat.

Hand out the Pipe Cleaner Creature Log in appendix G for each student to complete. This can be done as a draft before students get supplies to make the creature or after the students have finalized their design.

Play a game in which a few students place their creatures in their habitat while the other students are out of the area. Then have the students return and try to find the creatures. See which one is found first and which survived the longest, hidden from the "predators."

After the pipe cleaner creation, have students reflect on the success of their creature. Discuss with students how engineers reflect on their creations and are always looking for ways to improve their designs. Require reflections from students about how they could improve on their design if they were to do this activity again or other materials that they would like to have for a better creature.

21. Minecraft Science

Topic: Science in Video Games
Materials Needed: Minecraft computer game (Mojang Studios)
Vocabulary:

- Biome—ecological region
- Creeper—aggressive mob that tries to sneak up on a player before exploding
- Nether—a dimension filled with environmental hazards
- Mobs—all the creatures in the game
- Mod (modification)—anything that changes the content of the game
- Multiplayer—playing *Minecraft* with others on the internet

- Sandbox—a type of video game with an "open world" design where players can modify the game world and explore without restrictions of limitations. *Minecraft* is considered a sandbox game.
- Skin—any texture placed on an avatar or mob that allows the player to customize the game
- Spawn—the location where the player initially arrives in a new world
- Teleport (TP)—move quickly around the map

Literature Connections:

Mojang AB. *Minecraft: Maps; An Explorer's Guide to Minecraft*. Del Rey, 2019.
Mojang AB. *Minecraft for Beginners*. Del Rey, 2019.

Minecraft is a popular video game in which everything looks like it is made of blocks. There are no specific objectives. Players can work alone or with others to use the resources to build and craft whatever they desire and populate them with real or imaginary animals and people. The game encourages collaborative problem solving, persistence, compromise, communication, and creativity. Introduce the vocabulary words to students before playing the game.

An abundance of lessons using *Minecraft* have been created by educators and are available free of charge. Examples include: host a bridge-building competition across a ravine, use the material reducer to see what elements form common materials—then encourage students to complete a scavenger hunt to find materials that contain oxygen, and find a *Minecraft biome* and create a renewable energy source.[8]

Minecraft includes day- and nighttime cycles, climatically and geographically defined biomes, water in both solid and liquid states, lunar phases of the moon, coordinates to establish location, and various types of rocks. A teacher can use *Minecraft* to expose students to scientific concepts that relate to real-world experiences.[9]

NOTES

1. Keith M. Williamson, Lee Land, Beverly Butler, and Hassan B. Ndahi, "A Structured Framework for Using Games to Teach Mathematics and Science in K–12 Classrooms," *Technology Teacher* 64, no. 5 (2004): 15–18.
2. Yvette F. Greenspan, *A Guide to Teaching Elementary Science: Ten Easy Steps* (Boston: Sense, 2016), 45–46.

3. Margaret A. Honey and Margaret Hilton, eds., *Learning Science through Computer Games and Simulations* (Washington, DC: National Academies Press, 2011), 1–20.

4. Greenspan, *Guide to Teaching Elementary Science*, 72–73.

5. Adapted from the game "Catch Me If You Can: An Animal Needs Role-Play Game," by Eric A. Worch, Amy M. Scheuermann, and Jodi J. Haney, "Role-Play in the Science Classroom," *Science and Children* 47, no. 1 (2009): 54–59.

6. Adapted from lesson "Birds and Worms," by Project Learning Tree, *Project Learning Tree Pre K–8 Environmental Education Activity Guide* (4th ed.) (Washington, DC: American Forest Foundation, 2021): 111–12.

7. Adapted from lesson "Pipe Cleaner Animal Camouflage," by T. J. Fontaine, ECOS Inquiry Series, University of Montana, http://www.bioed.org/ECOS/inquiries/inquiries/FCCamo.pdf.

8. Minecraft Education Edition, accessed April 11, 2022, https://education.minecraft.net/en-us/resources/science-subject-kit.

9. Dan Brian Short, "Teaching Scientific Concepts Using a Virtual World—Minecraft," *Teaching Science* 58, no. 3 (2012): 55–58.

Chapter 3

Using Literature to Teach Science

In the busy world of the teacher, having the ability to build literacy skills while teaching content is a win-win scenario. It is expensive to supplement outdated textbooks, so why not use trade books to help fill in the gaps? Trade books can be defined as children's literature with curriculum content. Folktales, historical fiction, myths, and biographies can be considered trade books.

There is an abundance of trade books related to each area of science. For example, one relevant trade book to introduce information on weather is *Thunder Cake* (Polacco 1977). A grandmother eases a child's fear of thunderstorms by enlisting her help in baking a cake. After reading the book, teachers can share information from *Why Does Lightning Strike? Questions Children Ask about the Weather* (Martin 1996) and require students to do further research on weather phenomena. Then, as a class, make your own "thunder cake."

Illustration by Madalyn Stack.

Students are more likely to read science-based trade books on their own than a textbook. Teachers can use these books to introduce vocabulary, develop questions, define difficult concepts, and spark interest in science topics. Student attitudes toward science will be vastly improved through the use of literature.

While there is a plethora of science books available for teachers to use, some books can foster misconceptions. The National Science Teaching Association publishes an annual list of outstanding books appropriate for teaching science. Their criteria include: substantial science content; clear, accurate, and up-to-date information; clear distinctions between theories and facts; generalizations supported by facts; free of gender, ethnic, and socioeconomic bias.[1] Before using science trade books, teachers should check to see that illustrations are accurate and include labels, check the credentials of the author, and check to see that the text encourages scientific thinking.

Both nonfiction and fiction science books are an essential part of the elementary science class. Students learn that scientists research, gather data, experiment, and synthesize data. They can model this process through writing their own nonfiction literature. Students can research a topic, gather information, discern fact from opinion, and include maps, graphics, and diagrams in the book they write. Guidelines for writing nonfiction books include:[2]

- Use your district standards to guide your selection of a science topic for the unit.
- Select fiction picture books on that science topic, giving pairs of students their own book.
- Students will create three questions they have about the topic from reading the book that can guide their research.
- Provide extensive time for students to read a wide variety of nonfiction picture books and begin to find answers to their questions.
- Students will gather information, take notes, and conduct further science investigations to engage and learn about their science topic.
- Support your students' informational literacy with mini lessons on the differences between fiction and nonfiction, nonfiction text features, academic language, collecting research and writing notes, and author's purpose throughout the unit.

Students can read more than just a textbook to learn about science. Immersing them into fiction, nonfiction, poetry, folktales, picture books, novels, and informational books that promote self-selected reading can help supplement content from the textbook. The integration of literature and science enables teachers to generate interest and create a real-world context for understanding science content.[3]

The activities in this chapter will open up the world of science with literature. Reading is such an important part of the elementary curriculum. Incorporating cross-curricular material within the reading block is a great way to cover all the content that teachers are tasked with covering in a school year. The books included in this chapter can be used to cover English language arts (ELA) and science standards while presenting the content in a visually appealing, grade-level-appropriate way. Relatable characters, easy-to-follow plotlines, and attractive illustrations all help to interest students. Consideration was made in terms of diversity and inclusion with the books in this chapter.

Literature can be a springboard to ignite scientists' minds before, during, and after the instruction of content or completion of experiments. The five activities in this chapter provide ideas to use different types of literature to teach science (poetry, nonfiction, science fiction, constellation stories, fiction). Topics covered include: insect life cycles, space, star stories, rainbows, aliens, and UFOs.

ACTIVITIES FOR USING LITERATURE TO TEACH SCIENCE

22. Catch a Science Rhyme

Topic: Science in Poetry

Materials Needed: art supplies, science magazines or copies of science textbook pages

Vocabulary:

- Life cycle—series of stages an organism passes through as it matures
- Maturation—coming to full development

Literature Connections:

Fleischman, Paul. *Joyful Noise: Poems for Two Voices*. HarperCollins, 2019.
Florian, Douglas. *Comets, Stars, the Moon, and Mars: Space Poems and Paintings*. HMH Books for Young Readers, 2007.
Hopkins, Lee Bennett. *Spectacular Science: A Book of Poems*. Simon & Schuster Books for Young Readers, 2002.
Lewis, J. Patrick, and Laura Robb. *Poems for Teaching in the Content Areas: 75 Powerful Poems to Enhance Your History, Geography, Science, and Math Lessons*. Scholastic Teaching Resources, 2007.
Lionni, Leo. *Frederick*. Pantheon, 1967.
Scieszka, Jon. *Science Verse*. Viking Books for Young Readers, 2004.

Vardell, Sylvia, and Janet Wong. *The Poetry of Science: The Poetry Friday Anthology for Science for Kids*. Pomelo Books, 2015.

Winters, Kari-Lynn, and Lori Sherritt Fleming. *Hungry for Science: Poems to Crunch On*. Fitzhenry and Whiteside, 2018.

Poetry can be used in science to introduce vocabulary, explain content, and assess a unit of study. There are poems available from every area of science. With catchy rhythms and humor, poems are easily memorized by students and spark interest and curiosity in the classroom.

In the book *Joyful Noise: Poems for Two Voices* (Fleischman 2019), students learn about the *life cycles* and *maturation* of animals as they read as pairs and individuals throughout the poems. Assign partners and have the pairs practice reading the parts of the poems "Grasshoppers," "Honey Bees," and "Digger Wasps." Students take turns reading aloud in front of the class, then write a summary of the life cycle of their favorite poem from the book. You might even challenge your students to write their own two-voice poem.[4]

Share the book *Frederick* (Lionni 1967) with students. Frederick is a mouse that, instead of working with the other mice to gather food for winter, gathers images and words about nature. During the winter months when the food is gone, Frederick warms the other mice with his words and poem. Take students on a nature walk and ask them to record words and images in a notebook. Students can then write haiku nature poems with their words: the first line of five syllables, a second line of seven syllables, and a third line of five syllables.[5]

Art can be combined with poetry in the science classroom. Challenge students to "discover" a new planet to paint and write a poem about, following the examples in the book *Comets, Stars, the Moon, and Mars: Space Poems and Paintings* (Florian 2007). Another activity would be to copy a two-page spread from a science magazine, science textbook, or science fiction story. Students circle or highlight significant words; then paint a scene on the two pages that represents the content. Do not paint over the significant words.[6]

23. Constellation Stories

Topic: Star Stories
Materials Needed: umbrella, paper stars, oatmeal box or steel can, flashlight, paper, nail
Vocabulary:

- Constellation—configuration of stars used to organize a part of the sky
- Celestial coordinates—a grid system for locating things in the sky
- Galaxy—vast collection of stars, gas, and dust

- Milky Way—a faintly glowing band composed of billions of stars in our galaxy that contains our solar system
- Star—massive ball of gas

Literature Connections:

Ganeri, Anita. *Star Stories: Constellation Tales from around the World.* Running Press Kids, 2019.

Gillingham, Sara. *Seeing Stars: A Complete Guide to the 88 Constellations.* Phaidon, 2018.

Mitton, Jacqueline. *Once Upon a Starry Night: A Book of Constellations.* National Geographic Kids, 2009.

Simon, Seymour. *The Universe.* HarperCollins, 2006.

Pose questions to students: "Why is the sun a *star*?" "How many stars do you think are in the *galaxy*?" "How do we find specific stars?" (use *celestial coordinates*). "What galaxy do we live in?" (*Milky Way*).

Introduce students to star stories that various cultures have created. *Constellation* stories are a connection between science and culture. Elders and children sat around campfires imagining stories to tell. One such story explains how the Big Dipper changes position in the sky during the spring and summer seasons:

Never-Ending Bear Hunt

Many years ago, people looked into the night sky and imagined wonderful stories in the stars. One story lasts for a whole year, and tells about the adventures of the Great Bear and the Bird Hunters. When the winter ended, the Great Bear left her cave. She was very hungry after her long sleep, and she was anxious to find food. But as she hunted for food, other hunters were following her! Seven brave Bird Hunters followed the Great Bear across the sky. Robin led the hunt, followed closely by Chickadee and his cooking pot and Moose-bird. Farther behind were their friends: Pigeon, Blue Jay, Horned Owl, and Saw-whet. The bear looked big and clumsy, but she moved across the sky rapidly. The hunters followed behind all summer, but as autumn approached, they had still not caught up to the Great Bear. Some of the hunters became tired and discouraged. Saw-whet, the last hunter in line, left the hunt. Soon Horned Owl also gave up and went in search of Saw-whet. Blue Jay and Pigeon tried to keep up with the leaders, but soon they also left the hunt and flew home. Only Robin, Chickadee, and Moose-bird followed the Great Bear into the autumn. The bear grew angry and rose up on her hind legs. She growled loudly and clawed the air to scare the hunters. But Robin was a brave hunter. He shot an arrow and hit the Great Bear. Drops of her blood fell on Robin's feathers, turning his breast bright red. Other drops fell on the autumn leaves, coloring them a bright red. When winter came, the dead bear lay on her back up in the sky. But her spirit returned to the cave and entered another bear. In the spring, the bear will leave the cave again to travel across the spring and summer sky, always pursued by Bird Hunters.[7]

To accompany the story, glue paper stars onto the underside of an umbrella and twirl it slowly to demonstrate how the stars in the Northern Hemisphere appear to rotate around the North Star.[8] Then have students write their own constellation tale.

You can also use a cylindrical cardboard box, such as an oatmeal box, to project constellation images on the wall. Copy the constellation onto a sheet of thin paper and place the paper over the closed end of the round box. Punch holes with a nail through the star dots on the paper. In a dark room, shine a flashlight into the open end of the round box to throw an enlarged image of the constellation onto the wall. Rotate the box to see all positions of the constellation.[9]

24. Sky Colors

Topic: Rainbows
Materials Needed: prism, jar, water, milk, measuring spoon, flashlight, bubbles, 6 cups, food coloring, paper towels
Vocabulary:

- Horizontal—parallel to the ground
- Vertical—at right angle to the plane of the horizon
- Prism—three-dimensional solid used for dispersing or reflecting light

Literature Connections:

Clevenger, Bill. *Why the Sky Is Blue & Other Wonders of the Earth.* Bdd Promotional Book, 1992.
Gerson, Mary-Joan. *Why the Sky Is Far Away: A Nigerian Folktale.* Little, Brown Books for Young Readers, 1995.
Kramer, Stephen P. *Theodoric's Rainbow.* W. H. Freeman, 1995.

Post questions for students: "How does the sky change color?" "Where does the sky start and stop?" Share and discuss the book *Why the Sky Is Far Away: A Nigerian Folktale* (Gerson 1995). Ask students to make predictions as to why the sky changes colors. Use the *prism* to show the rainbow colors from sunlight. Fill the jar with water and observe the colors of light when the sun or bright light shines through. Add 2 teaspoons of milk to the water and stir. Shine the flashlight *vertically* into the mixture and observe the water, then *horizontally*. Ask students to identify the colors.[10] Finish the lesson by reading *Why the Sky Is Blue & Other Wonders of the Earth* (Clevenger 1992).

Challenge students to answer: "How many ways can you create a rainbow?" Explore prisms, water and mirrors, paints, language, and legends. Read *Theodoric's Rainbow* (Kramer 1995), a picture book that relates attitudes of science with the love of rainbows.[11] Take the students outside on a sunny day to blow bubbles and examine the rainbow colors.

In the classroom, place six cups in a circle and fill every other cup with water. In the cups of water add red, blue, and yellow food coloring. Roll up six pieces of paper towels to make tubes and place the tubes from one cup to the next. Be sure the cups are arranged red, empty, yellow, empty, blue, empty. During the day, the water will "walk" on the towels, so that red water will mix with yellow water to make orange, yellow with blue to make green, and blue with red to make purple.[12]

25. Universe of Reading[13]

Topic: Space in Books

Materials Needed: newspaper articles on space events, poems about space, space posters, paintings about space, rocket models, books and music connected to space

Vocabulary:

- Asteroid—rocky object that moves in an orbit around the sun
- Meteor—small piece of matter that enters the earth's atmosphere and burns brightly
- Light-year—the distance that light travels in one year, moving at about 186,000 miles per second
- Black hole—place in space thought to be caused by the collapse of a massive star

Literature Connections:

Cameron, Eleanor. *The Wonderful Flight to the Mushroom Planet.* Little, Brown Books for Young Readers, 1988.

Gibbs, Stuart. *Space Case (Moon Base Alpha).* Simon & Schuster Books for Young Readers, 2015.

Hirst, Robin, and Sally Hirst. *My Place in Space.* Orchard Books, 1992.

L'Engle, Madeleine. *A Wrinkle in Time.* Farrar, Straus and Giroux, 2010.

MacGregor, Ellen. *Miss Pickerell Goes to Mars.* Scholastic Books, 1961.

Walsh, Jill Paton. *The Green Book.* Square Fish, 2012.

Williams, Jay, and Raymond Abrashkin. *Danny Dunn and the Anti-gravity Planet.* Wildside, 2015.

Yolen, Jane. *Commander Toad in Space.* Puffin Books, 1987.

Set up a "space travel" center in the classroom for students to explore. Musical selections could include "The Planets" (Gustav Holst 1918), "Rocket Man" (Elton John 1972), and "Space Oddity" (David Bowie 1999). Trade books could include *StarTalk: Everything You Ever Need to Know about Space Travel, Sci-Fi, the Human Race, the Universe, and Beyond* (Tyson 2019), *The Complete Guide to Space Exploration* (Lonely Planet Kids 2020), and *Do Your Ears Pop in Space? And 500 Other Surprising Questions about Space Travel* (Mullane 1997).

Allow students time to browse materials, write their reflections, and then come back together to process what they learned. Assign students the vocabulary words to find in the materials: *asteroid, meteor, light-year, black hole*. Students could use the Knew-New Chart from the "Templates to Use during Activities" section in the "Resources" chapter of this book to jot down things they already knew before visiting the center, and things they learned afterward.

26. Sci-Fi Reality

Topic: Aliens and UFOs
Materials Needed: books about aliens and UFOs, materials to dramatize or make sound effects for radio show
Vocabulary:

- UFO—unidentified flying object
- Phenomena—extraordinary occurrences or events
- Science fiction—genre of fiction that deals with futuristic concepts
- Alien—a creature from outer space
- Extraterrestrial—an alien from another planet
- AI—artificial intelligence; computer-based intelligence
- Dystopian—a dangerous future world
- Postapocalyptic—after a world-changing event, like a nuclear war
- Propaganda—false information to influence the public
- Surveillance—closely watching the behavior of a person or creature
- Cyborg—part machine, part robot creature
- Android—robot that looks and acts like a person

Literature Connections:

Cline, Ernest. *Ready Player One*. Ballantine Books, 2011.
Corey, James S. A. *Leviathan Awakes: The Expanse Book 1*. Orbit, 2011.
Dennett, Preston. *Schoolyard UFO Encounters: 100 True Accounts*. Blue Giant Books, 2019.
Hughes, Monica. *Invitation to the Game*. Simon & Schuster Children's, 1991.

McCarthy, Megan. *Aliens Are Coming! The True Account of the 1938 War of the Worlds Radio Broadcast.* Dragonfly Books, 2009.
McNamara, Margaret. *The Three Little Aliens and the Big Bad Robot.* Schwartz and Wade, 2011.

Science fiction books speak to social and political aspects of life. Books by authors like Madeleine L'Engle, H. G. Wells, and George Orwell have created futuristic worlds that spark our imaginations—with robots, artificial intelligence (AI), and spaceships. Young people can see themselves in this genre—coping and surviving. To them, science fiction represents their future. Many science fiction books have been turned into major motion pictures or television series, such as *Leviathan Awakes: The Expanse Book 1* (Corey 2011) and *Ready Player One* (Cline 2011). Read the books with students; then show the movies and evaluate the differences from the books. Ask students: "Which books represent *dystopian* societies?" "Which books represent *postapocalyptic* events?" "Could you survive in either of these representations?"

Although science fiction may be loosely based on science, it is important to remind students that it is still fiction. You should have discussions with students about whether the story could really happen in today's world or if it might be make-believe. Ask students to read and discuss science fiction texts and then conduct research to find facts that support or dispute what they read. Ask students how the information they found might change the plot of the story. Discuss with students the difference between a *cyborg*, an *android*, and a robot.

Share the book *Schoolyard UFO Encounters: 100 True Accounts* (Dennett 2019). Have students investigate "Project Blue Book," a program sponsored by the United States Air Force to examine UFO sightings from 1952 through 1969. From 1947 to 1969, there were more than twelve thousand sightings reported to the air force, with 701 remaining "unidentified." Most were identified as natural *phenomena* or aircraft. Ask students to debate whether they believe *aliens* exist and justify their statements.

Talk to students about life before television when radio was the main source for information and entertainment. Read the book *Aliens Are Coming! The True Account of the 1938 War of the Worlds Radio Broadcast* (McCarthy 2009). Tell students that because there was no way to verify information, many people who heard the broadcast really believed it, and some even began to panic. Ask students: "Was the radio show a form of *propaganda*?" Have students discuss what they might have done as a listener in this situation. Have students write and dramatize their own radio show.[14]

NOTES

1. Christine Anne Royce, Emily Morgan, and Karen Ansberry, "Why Use Trade Books to Teach Science?," in *Teaching Science through Trade Books* (Arlington, VA: National Science Teachers Association 2012), 5–9.

2. Sara Kersten, "Becoming Nonfiction Authors: Engaging in Science Inquiry," *Reading Teacher* 71, no. 1 (2017): 33–41, https://doi.org/10.1002/trtr.1577.

3. William P. Bintz, Pam Wright, and Julie Sheffer, "Using Copy Change with Trade Books to Teach Earth Science," *Reading Teacher* 64, no. 2 (2010): 106–19.

4. "Why Use Poetry in Your Science Classroom?," *Teacher's Workstation* (blog), March 20, 2016, https://teachersworkstation.com/2016/03/20/why-use-poetry-in -your-science-classroom/#:~:text=Poetry%20is%20a%20great%20tool,for%20kids %20learning%20to%20read.

5. Carole Cox, "Literature-Based Teaching in Science," *Reading Rockets* (blog), accessed February 3, 2022, https://www.readingrockets.org/article/literature-based -teaching-science-poetry-walks.

6. Dimitra Neonakis, "Creating Poetry from Non-fiction Text," *Think Fun: Ignite Your Mind!* (blog), February 28, 2019, http://info.thinkfun.com/stem-education/ creating-poetry-from-science-and-nonfiction-text.

7. Project ARTIST, "Never-Ending Bear Hunt," University of Arizona, accessed March 3, 2022, http://www.u.arizona.edu/~lebofsky/bear.htm.

8. Sandy Kaser, "Searching the Heavens with Children's Literature: A Design for Teaching Science," *Language Arts* 78, no. 4 (2001): 348–56.

9. Adapted from lesson "Oatmeal Box Planetarium," by Martin Gardner, *Entertaining Science Experiments with Everyday Objects* (New York: Dover, 1981), 16.

10. Adapted from lesson "Why Is the Sky Blue—Easy Science Projects," by Science Made Simple, accessed April 12, 2023, https://www.sciencemadesimple.com/ blue_sky_science_projects.html.

11. Kaser, "Searching the Heavens with Children's Literature."

12. Adapted from lesson "Rainbow Ideas," by Greg Smedley-Warren, *The Kindergarten Smorgasboard* (blog), April 4, 2017, https://thekindergartensmorgasboard.com /2017/04/rainbow-week-ideas.html.

13. Kaser, "Searching the Heavens with Children's Literature."

14. Adapted from lesson "Aliens Are Coming!," by Kristen Goode, Study.com, accessed March 2, 2022, https://study.com/academy/lesson/aliens-are-coming-lesson -plan.html.

Chapter 4

Using Music to Teach Science

Early scientists saw music as an integral part of science. Pythagoras, Galileo, and Newton all sought to explain the universe's connection to music.[1] Music is not just an arrangement of pitches to entertain us, but also a bridge across cultures and languages. Music is emotion that is clustered into genres, such as love songs, religious songs, healing songs, and lullabies.[2]

Songs can serve as a mnemonic device to help students retain information. Remember learning the alphabet from the ABC song? Science songs can help improve recall by organizing information into patterns. Students can relate to song lyrics and are more likely to discuss science outside of class when the concepts are contained in a song. Music is believed to act as a calming influence to reduce anxiety in students. Put on quiet background music to provide comfort and a sense of safety in the classroom. By accompanying music with

Illustration by Madalyn Stack.

visuals or body movement, teachers can reach several learning styles at once and provide a boost of energy during lengthy class periods.

There are places where teachers can find prewritten science songs for classroom use. The database Sing about Science and Math has a search engine for more than seven thousand songs. The Grammy-winning band They Might Be Giants produced a CD called *Here Comes Science* (Disney Sound/Idlewild 2009). Songs from the album include: "Science Is Real," "How Many Planets," "Speed and Velocity," and "Waves." The Banana Slug String Band posts environmental education songs (https://www.bananaslugstringband .com/), such as "Dirt Made My Lunch" and "Pollinator Nation." Other science songs can be obtained from Science Songs for Teaching (https://www .songsforteaching.com/sciencesongs.htm), and Elementary Science Songs for Kids (https://www.science4us.com/science-songs/).

Encourage students to write their own science songs. There are criteria available to guide students in songwriting: Have the students work in small groups to allow them to specialize according to their abilities and comfort zones. Establish the criteria for grading in advance. Will students be scored on their singing ability? Does the song contain accurate information? Are the melody and rhythm fitting? Is the song compelling and interesting to listen to?[3]

Whether teachers use mainstream songs or student-/teacher-written songs, the educational benefits abound. Spontaneously bursting into song will definitely catch the attention of students! Teachers do need to remember that creating lyrics to a copyrighted song is okay by law, as long as these songs are in the context of the classroom and not performed for the public.[4]

The activities in this chapter activate students' auditory cortexes by using musical instruments and songs. Using music in the classroom helps students to retain information by presenting it in a different mode of delivery. These activities introduce students to vocabulary within the concept of sound and have them think about the sounds around them in the context of nature's music. Students are encouraged to see patterns in the natural environment and investigate how humans use these vibrations in a way that is pleasing and entertaining.

Music can help to appeal to students who don't at first see themselves as scientists by integrating science and the arts. The five activities in this chapter include ideas on how to use music to teach science. Topics covered include: rock cycles, insects, music vibrations, music pitch, science in Broadway songs, and communication with drums.

ACTIVITIES FOR USING MUSIC TO TEACH SCIENCE

27. Sing a Song of Science

Topic: Science in Music
Materials Needed: none
Vocabulary:

- Tune—the melody
- Tempo—the speed
- Rhythm—the beat

Literature Connections:

Cross, Alan. *The Science of Song: How and Why We Make Music.* Kids Can, 2021.
Harmon, Sharon A. *Horatio Mortimer Loved Music.* Diane Kane, 2020.
Kadarusman, Michelle. *Music for Tigers.* Pajama, 2021.
Lithgow, John. *Never Play Music Right Next to the Zoo.* Simon & Schuster Books for Young Readers, 2013.

Pose the question to students: "How does a song sound different when you make a change (e.g., sing faster or slower, sing louder or softer, sing higher or lower)?" Introduce students to the concepts of *tempo* and *rhythm*. Have students identify items in nature that might make a rhythmic sound (e.g., waves on a beach, crickets chirping). Tell students that the frequency (tempo) of the chirping of a cricket varies with the temperature outside.

Take familiar *tunes* and change the words to science concepts. Children will sing along with something known to them and have fun learning about science in the process! Sing the song below to the tune of "Row, Row, Row Your Boat":

Rock Cycles[5]

SEDIMENTARY rock
Has been formed in layers
Often found near water sources
With fossils from decayers.
Then there's IGNEOUS rock
Here since Earth was born
Molten Lava, cooled and hardened
That's how it is formed.
These two types of rocks
Can also be transformed
With pressure, heat and chemicals
METAMORPHIC they'll become.

Another familiar tune is "Head, Shoulders, Knees, and Toes." Use the song for these words to teach students about the parts of an insect:

Insect Parts[6]

Head (Point to head.)
Thorax (Point to chest.)
Abdomen—abdomen! (Point to stomach.)
Head, thorax, abdomen—abdomen!
And eyes (Point to eyes.)
And mouth (Point to mouth.)
And antennae, two (Stick 2 fingers up.)
Six legs (Wiggle 3 fingers on each hand.)
And there's an insect for you! (Leave off a verse each time you sing and hum.)

28. Good Vibrations

Topic: Music Vibrations
Materials Needed: shakers, various types of drums, drumsticks, rhythm sticks, rain sticks, combs, wax paper, oatmeal boxes, cigar boxes, rubber bands, paper plates, dried beans, paper towel tubes, rocks, sticks, pans, wooden spoons, straws, shoeboxes
Vocabulary:

- Vibration—rapid, oscillating movement that causes sound
- Treble clef—symbol placed on music staff to show the notes above middle C that will be sung or played
- Bass clef—symbol placed on a music staff to show the F below middle C; often indicates the left-hand notes when playing a piano

Literature Connections:

Kenney, Karen Latchana. *Buzzing Breath (The Physics of Music).* Cantata Learning, 2019.
Richards, Mary, and David Schweitzer. *A History of Music for Children.* Thames & Hudson, 2021.
Thaler, Mike. *The Music Teacher from the Black Lagoon.* Scholastic, 2000.
Weber, Vicky. *Rhythm Rescue.* Trunk Up Books, 2020.
Weber, Vicky. *When Step Met Skip.* Trunk Up Books, 2021.

Talk about thunderstorms with students and the sounds they may hear in the storm (sprinkling rain, hard rain, thunder, wind). Have students choose instruments (shakers, drums, rhythm sticks, rain sticks) or make instruments that can make the sounds of a thunderstorm.[7] Create a thunderstorm gradually commencing, then getting louder and louder, and finally fading away.

Provide students with a variety of materials to create an instrument: combs, wax paper, oatmeal boxes, cigar boxes, rubber bands, paper plates, dried beans, paper towel tubes, rocks, sticks, pans, wooden spoons, straws, shoeboxes. Have students accompany recorded music with their handmade instruments or create their own musical piece. Ask students: "How do the different materials affect the sound?" Have students classify the instrument sounds (e.g., metal instruments sound like . . . ; paper instruments sound like . . .).[8]

Tell students that on a music staff, *treble clefs* are used for higher-sounding notes and *bass clefs* are used for lower-sounding notes. Ask students to determine which of the materials they created would be written on a treble clef line and which on a bass clef line. Inform students that the faster the *vibration*, the higher the note. The slower the vibration, the lower the note.

Create instrument centers. For example, a drum table can include various types of African drums and drumsticks. Beat the different drums to distinguish between sounds. Place dried beans on a drum before striking, and talk about vibrations. Place beads, beans, or rocks in bottles and note the different sounds. Introduce shaking instruments, like maracas and tambourines.[9]

Ask students: "Why do we find some sounds pleasing while others are distressing?" Have students list sounds that they hate to hear (e.g., fingers scraping a chalkboard, baby crying, electric drill, squeaky brakes) and sounds they like to hear (e.g., baby laughing, rain, applause). Evolution and our own experiences have wired our brains to react to certain frequencies.[10] You may play a variety of sounds and let students do a thumbs-up or thumbs-down as to whether they enjoy the sounds.

29. Pitch Perfect[11]

Topic: Music Pitch
Materials Needed: electronic tuner, 8 glasses, water, spoons (1 metal, 1 wooden, 1 plastic), piano, music—"The Planets" by Gustav Holst
Vocabulary:

- Pitch—classification of how high or low a note is when played or sung
- Range—distance from the lowest to highest pitch a person can sing or an instrument can play
- Harmony—what occurs when more than one note is played or sung at a time
- Harmonic interval—measurement between two pitches in scale steps
- Tone—quality of sound

- Scale—ordered sequence of notes from which you can build melodies and harmonies

Literature Connections:

Christie, Tory. *Curious McCarthy's Not-So-Perfect Pitch*. Picture Window Books, 2017.
National Geographic Kids. *Turn It Up! A Pitch-Perfect History of Music That Rocked the World*. National Geographic Kids, 2019.
Reeves, Betty M. *Melody Street: Story and Illustrations*. Betty's Music, 2018.
Spilsbury, Louise, and Richard Spilsbury. *Why Can't I Hear That? Pitch and Frequency (Exploring Sound)*. Raintree, 2014.

It was Pythagoras who discovered that musical intervals are based on mathematical ratios that, amazingly, appear in astronomy. *Harmonic intervals* are composed of two *pitches*, each with a specific vibrating frequency. An E on the top space of a music staff vibrates at 660 cycles per second. An A below the E vibrates at 440 cycles per second. The ratio of 660/440 is equal to 3/2, the mathematical ratio that defines a perfect fifth in music. Pythagoras believed that the seven heavenly bodies visible to the naked eye (sun, moon, Mercury, Venus, Mars, Jupiter, Saturn) rotated around Earth on seven concentric spheres. Each sphere emitted a *tone*, and all seven together created a celestial *harmony*.

The astronomer Ptolemy matched pitches to twelve constellations, rather than the planets. An Islamic scholar, Al Hasan al Katib, also connected music to the zodiac, pointing out that twelve is easily divisible into halves, thirds, and fourths, and forms the perfect intervals in music.

Isaac Newton describes the similarity of the gravitational force to the effect of tension on the strings of a musical instrument. German astronomer Johannes Kepler suggested that planets "sing" a *range* of notes, depending on their speed.

Ask students: "Which planets would have low pitches and which high pitches?" Assign each student a planet and have them stand around the sun in distance order. Have students rotate around the sun in a clockwise direction, the closer planets rotating faster. Collaborate with the music teacher to play the pitch and range for each planet as they rotate: Saturn 5:4 (lower notes on staff, bass clef—G, A, B, A, G); Jupiter 6:5 (lower notes on staff, bass clef—G, A, B flat, A, G); Mars 3:2 (upper notes on staff, bass clef—F, G, A, B flat, C, B flat, A, G, F); Earth 16:15 (middle notes on staff, treble clef—G, A flat, G); Venus 1:1 (upper notes on staff, treble clef—E, E, E); and Mercury 12:5 (middle notes on staff, treble clef—A, B, C, D, E, F, G, A, B, C, B, A, G, F,

E, D, C, B, A). Have students listen to the pitches without the movements and identify each of the planets. Play "The Planets" (Gustav Holst 1918) and have students guess which planet the music represents.

Ask students: "Does a low C have the same vibrations per second as a high C?" Have students watch an electronic tuner that shows Hz (cycles per second) as a musician plays various notes. Talk about how radio waves, sound waves, and electrical signals in computers all have frequency (the number of waves that pass through a space in a given amount of time).

Fill eight glasses with various amounts of water. Experiment with how each glass sounds when you hit it with a spoon. Students will learn quickly that glasses with less water have a lower pitch. Have students experiment with different types of glass tappers: metal spoon, wooden spoon, plastic spoon. Which one makes the clearest sound? Try different types of glasses to see which makes the best sound. Slightly wet your finger and gently glide it around the edge of the glass to produce a higher-sounding frequency. This experiment works best with crystal.

Talk about how the size of an instrument and the amount of air blowing through it can affect pitch. Examine the many different ways in which instruments produce vibrations—by plucking or bowing a string, buzzing the lips in a mouthpiece, vibrating a reed, hitting a surface, scraping an object, and so on.

30. Broadway and Science

Topic: Science in Music
Materials Needed: various Broadway tunes
Vocabulary:

- Genre—the style of something (e.g., drama, comedy, tragedy, pop rock, classical)
- Improvisation—something made up on the spot
- Projection—the volume in which you speak or sing
- Callback—a second audition
- Dress rehearsals—the final rehearsals done for a show in full makeup and costume
- Downstage—the section of stage nearest the audience

Literature Connections:

Allman, John Robert. *B Is for Broadway: Onstage and Backstage from A to Z.* Doubleday Books for Young Readers, 2022.
Amaker, Marcus. *Black Music Is.* Free Verse, 2021.
Hopgood, Tim. *Singing in the Rain.* Henry Holt, 2017.

Timbers, Alex. *Broadway Bird*. Feiwel & Friends, 2022.
Yacka, Douglas. *Where Is Broadway?* Penguin Workshop, 2019.

Musicals tell stories through song, and many of the songs relate to science. Introduce students to the *genre* of Broadway songs. In the musical *Something Rotten*, two playwrights are competing with William Shakespeare. The opening number "Welcome to the Renaissance" describes advances in the sciences and new innovations during the time period. The entrepreneur Henry Ford earns a song in the musical *Ragtime* about the impact of the assembly line. The entertaining song "The Wells Fargo Wagon" in *The Music Man* features the convenience of a new transportation system.[12]

There are many Broadway productions that connect to science and science fiction: *Young Frankenstein* (Mel Brooks 2007), *A New Brain* (William Finn 2002), *Back to the Future: The Musical* (Robert Zemeckis and Bob Gale 2020), and *Little Shop of Horrors* (Howard Ashman 2003) are just a few examples. You may encourage your students to write their own Broadway production of a science unit and perform for an audience. Another idea is to assign the same topic to groups of students, but have them write a song in different genres: pop, rock, country, hip-hop, techno, or even classical.

Introduce a new concept in science by playing a Broadway song prior to class. It can stir up student interest in the lesson the moment they arrive. Or, play the song during class, ask a question about the science concept embedded within the song, then allow students to pair/share their answers. Additionally, assign the song outside of class and have students complete a written assignment, or choose their own song that would go along with the unit lessons.[13]

Introduce students to Broadway terms: *improvisation, projection, callback, dress rehearsals, downstage*. Have students research ways in which the theater and science connect. For example, the construction of theaters and sets require engineering thought. Mechanical devices have been invented for theatrical effects. Stage lighting highlights actors and establishes moods, and has made theaters safer from fires.[14]

31. Talking Drums

Topic: Communication through Drumming
Materials Needed: balloons, bowls, scissors, set of 8-inch embroidery hoops, 2 medium-sized plastic planting pots, clear duct tape, decorative duct tape, glue, ribbon, pencils, empty oatmeal boxes

Vocabulary:

- Percussion—musical instruments played by striking with the hand or a beater
- Rhythm—repeated pattern of sound
- Pitch—high or low note sounds

Literature Connections:

Nwalie, Angela. *The Twenty-Six Talking Drums*. Lulu, 2020.
Price, Christine. *Talking Drums of Africa*. Atheneum, 1973.
Unobagha, Uzo. *Off to the Sweet Shores of Africa*. Chronicle Books, 2006.

Traditionally, drum *rhythms* and their dances would have been associated with specific occasions, with each rhythm having a time and place. For example, an ancient dance common for women in West Africa centers around the movement of pounding millet with a mortar and pestle. Drums were often used as a means of communication over long distances in many African countries. Some drums could be heard as far as seven miles away. A drum could be as tall as ten feet or small enough to hold in one hand. A "talking drum" was often made from a special tree that grew by the side of roads and paths where people often walked.

Native Americans used drums in communal activities, in shamanic magic, and as part of their ceremonies. Some tribes believed that beating the drums allowed communication with the spirits and got the attention of their gods. The beats carried prayers for healing. Large drums were used in powwows to guide singing and dancing.

An instrument is often thought to be "alive" and makes its own language. The skin of goats (the most talkative of animals) is used exclusively in making drums in the country of Senegal. In particular, the *tama* is a talking drum whose *pitch* can be regulated by squeezing the strings that surround the drum with the arm, which raises the pitch and imitates the inflections of human voice. Squeezing the drum changes the tension of the cords that attach to the two drum heads.

The action of hitting a *percussion* instrument with hands, mallets, sticks, or brushes produces different sounds at different volumes. The skin of the drum vibrates when hit. As the air molecules vibrate against each other, sound waves are formed, and the sound of the drums can be heard. The pitch of a drum depends on how tight its skin is. If the skin is tight, the drum makes a high note; if it is slack, it makes a low note. Air inside a drum also influences its pitch. The more air in a drum, the lower the note. The less air in a drum, the higher the note.

Ask students to research the various types of materials used to make drums. Using scissors, have students cut off the end of a balloon and stretch the balloon over a bowl. An empty oatmeal box can also be used. Experiment with hitting the homemade drum with hands, pencils, or other objects to determine the difference in sound. Students can make their own "talking drum" by following the directions below:[15]

Cover each pot with two layers of clear duct tape. Glue the bottoms of the planting pots together. Secure one embroidery hoop to the top of each side of the drum using the decorative duct tape. Attach the ribbon to the hoops to serve as a shoulder strap. Have students create rhythms with a pencil to represent various words or phrases.

Talking drums have been called different names throughout Africa: *dondo, tamanin, donno, kalangu, igba, doodo, gangan.* Using the chart in appendix H, ask students to examine other types of drums and evaluate their use as a talking drum: snare, bass, tenor, timpani, congas, bongos, djembe.

NOTES

1. George L. Rogers, "The Music of the Spheres: Cross-Curricular Perspectives on Music and Science," *National Association for Music Education* 103, no. 1 (2016): 41–48, https://doi.org/10.1177/0027432116654547.

2. Kim Armstrong, "How Sound Becomes Music," *Association for Psychological Science* (blog), April 30, 2019, https://www.psychologicalscience.org/observer/how-sound-becomes-music.

3. Gregory Crowther, "Using Science Songs to Enhance Learning: An Interdisciplinary Approach," *Life Sciences Education* 11 (2012): 26–30.

4. Crowther, "Using Science Songs to Enhance Learning."

5. University of Arkansas Center for Math and Science Education, "Rock Cycle Song," accessed March 4, 2022, https://cmase.uark.edu/_resources/pdf/gems/rock_cycle_song.pdf.

6. "Insects Body," from *Songs for Teaching*, accessed March 4, 2022, https://songsforteaching.com/drjean/kissbrain_s/16insectsbody.pdf.

7. Jessica Peresta, "Music and Science Integration Ideas for Kids," *The Domestic Musician* (blog), accessed March 4, 2022, https://www.thedomesticmusician.com/music-and-science-integration-ideas-for-kids/.

8. Maia Hamann, "Teaching Science in Music Class," *Your Classical* (blog), March 19, 2015, https://www.classicalmpr.org/blog/classical-notes/2015/03/19/teaching-science-in-music-class.

9. Carol Seefeldt, "Teaching Science through the Visual Arts and Music," *Scholastic Early Childhood Today* 18, no. 6 (2004): 29–34.

10. Sevak Kirakosyan, "How Frequencies Work: Less Science, More Fun," *Musical U* (blog), accessed March 3, 2022, https://www.musical-u.com/learn/how-frequencies-work-less-science-more-fun/.

11. Rogers, "Music of the Spheres."

12. Matthew C. Rousu, "Using Show Tunes to Teach about Free (and Not-So-Free) Markets," *Journal of Private Enterprise* 33, no. 4 (2018): 111–28.

13. Rousu, "Using Show Tunes to Teach."

14. Kay DeMetz, "Toward a Synthesis of Science and Theatre Arts," *Forum on Public Policy* 2007, no. 1 (2007): 1–13.

15. Adapted from lesson "Instruments! West African Talking Drum," from MIM Kids, accessed October 28, 2022, http://www.mim.org/wp-content/uploads/2017/02/2014-05-13-MIMkids-West-African-Talking-Drum_v3.pdf.

Chapter 5

Using the Community and the Natural Environment to Teach Science

Teachers need to help students understand that science permeates our surroundings. Create an interest in learning science using the playground, neighborhood, parks, forests, or nearby fields. There you can compare and contrast different types of bark and leaves, take samples of pond water for organisms, observe and compare vegetation in sunlit versus dark forested areas, or learn from professionals at a nature center about plants and animals. Children learn by using their senses; therefore, it seems logical to use the natural environment as a learning tool.

The 5E (engage, explore, explain, elaborate, evaluate) instructional model works well in an outdoor setting.[1] To generate interest and curiosity

Illustration by Madalyn Stack.

(engagement stage), assess student prior knowledge and introduce further information on the topic. For example, ask students to write on a chart their ideas for "What is soil?," "Where can you find soil?," and "What animals live in soil?" Read *Dirt: The Scoop on Soil* (Rosinsky 2002) to students and ask them to revisit the chart and see what changes they would make.

Allow students time to work together with materials and tools to investigate their surroundings (exploration stage). Ask probing questions to guide students with their investigations. For example, give students small shovels, strainers, and buckets and have students dig in a plot of soil and uncover earthworms. Ask students to speculate on the question: "Do worms eat dirt?" or "What do worms eat?"

Ask students to explain in their own words their discoveries (explanation stage); then the teacher can provide a more scientific explanation. For example, ask students: "How does an earthworm help farmers?" Students might say that worms dig holes for seeds to go in. The teacher can explain that earthworms loosen and enrich the soil and increase the water-holding capacity.

Next, students can apply what they have learned into new situations (elaboration stage). Encourage students to think about what ants or bugs do with soil and how they could help build a home for them. As they do so, the teacher will observe and assess the students' ability to apply new skills or concepts (evaluation stage).

In the teaching of science, students should be allowed the opportunity to infer, predict, and observe the natural environment. For example, students could examine cells in a microscope from objects picked up on a nature walk, draw the veins of a leaf and study the parts of a flower, listen to the sounds of birds and insects in an outdoor habitat, observe camouflage patterns of animals in a field or forest, or photograph the changing seasons.

To encourage scientific discovery in the natural environment, teachers need to collect supplies and materials for students to use. Some examples include: field journals, flashlights, insect repellent, rain gear, meter wheel, surveyor flags, camera, GPS device, magnifying lenses, containers, clipboards, nets, and digging implements. Students should have a good background knowledge of the content to be explored, submit one or more investigative questions, pose a hypothesis, identify variables to be measured or observed, and keep a detailed field journal.

It is important that teachers instruct students on safety procedures[2] before spending time in nature:

- Avoid poison oak and poison ivy, as you may get an itchy rash. These plants can be recognized by their clusters of three leaves ("Leaves of three, let it be").

- Stay back from beehives and wasp and hornet nests. These insects are protective of their homes and can give painful stings. Check to see if students have allergies to bee stings.
- Watch out for long grass or woodpiles where snakes could be hiding. Learn to identify venomous snakes in your area.
- Avoid stepping on anthills, as some ants bite and sting.
- Look carefully in caves and large homes that may be home to a wild animal. It is possible that the animal may be at home.
- Don't eat unidentified berries or mushrooms from the wild, as many are poisonous.
- Wear bug spray and check for ticks after spending time outside.
- Be careful of deep or fast-moving water.

Within the community, teachers can give students the opportunity to visit a science museum, science center, aquarium, garden, nature center, or zoo as part of the learning process. This gives students access to innovative resources and allows hands-on learning of material taught in class. In addition, students can explore places that are unique to their area, such as a creek, pond, river, city street, or even people of the community. Field trips should be a regular part of the curriculum, if allowed by the school. In some cases, virtual field trips or outreach programs are available where funding and transportation are not readily available to schools.

Community resources can be unconventional sites: a local farm, a hardware store, an urban playground, a factory. Neighborhood habitats allow students to discover science in familiar settings. Most importantly, teachers should visit each site to determine how the resources fit within the science curriculum and meet the students' cognitive levels. Teachers should plan pre- and post-activities as well.[3]

By involving students in outdoor learning, teachers will pique the curiosity of students, integrate inquiry learning and critical thinking skills, and help students develop an appreciation of nature and respect for living things. Teachers need to provide guidance and a set of standards on how data should be gathered, recorded, and reported. Also, provide information on the sampling protocol and make site visits ahead of time. Protected areas such as state parks, zoos, and wetlands make ideal places for field studies and often have education outreach systems in place.

The activities in this chapter encourage students to explore their community and the greater world around them. Getting students outside the four walls of the classroom is an instant engagement technique. Many schools are situated on tracts of land that include fields, patches of grass, greenways, and the increasingly popular outdoor classrooms. However, even schools that don't have an abundance of natural outdoor spaces tend to have playground areas with organic environments. Teachers needn't look much farther than outside their own school building to find themselves and their students immersed in nature.

The activities in this chapter provide teachers with ways to get students outdoors and learning science. Activities use everything from grassy areas to the sun or the weather that surrounds us, even in the most urban communities. The seven activities in this chapter provide ideas on using the community and the natural environment to teach science. Topics covered include: ecosystems, weather measurement, identifying scat, making a solar oven, zoo scavenger hunt, point and nonpoint source pollution, and wildlife scavenger hunt.

ACTIVITIES FOR USING THE COMMUNITY AND THE NATURAL ENVIRONMENT TO TEACH SCIENCE

32. Ruining an Ecosystem[4]

Topic: Ecosystems
Materials Needed: black, green, and red stickers; note cards; string
Vocabulary:

- Ecosystem—a group of living organisms and the physical environment with which they interact
- Wetland—an ecosystem defined by the presence of water
- Old-growth forest—complex, biodiverse forest at least 150 years old
- Biodiversity—variety of living organisms on all levels

Literature Connections:

Arnold, Tedd. *Dirty Gert*. Holiday House, 2014.

Batten, Mary. *Aliens from Earth: When Animals and Plants Invade Other Ecosystems*. Peachtree, 2016.

Cherry, Lynne. *The Great Kapok Tree: A Tale of the Amazon Rain Forest*. HMH Books for Young Readers, 2000.

Franco, Betsy. *Pond Circle*. Margaret K. McElderry Books, 2009.

Gholz, Sophia. *The Boy Who Grew a Forest: The True Story of Jadav Payeng*. Sleeping Bear, 2019.

Isabella, Jude. *Bringing Back the Wolves: How a Predator Restored an Ecosystem*. Kids Can, 2020.

Love, Jason Patrick. *Shady Streams, Slippery Salamanders*. Muddy Boots, 2019.

McNulty, F. *How to Dig a Hole to the Other Side of the World*. HarperCollins, 1995.

Nolan, T. *Rocks Don't Just Sit There*. McGraw-Hill, 1994.

Rosinsky, Natalie Myra. *Dirt: The Scoop on Soil*. Picture Window Books, 2002.

Silver, Donald. *African Savanna*. McGraw-Hill, 1997.

Silver, Donald. *Pond*. McGraw-Hill, 1997.

Silverstein, Shel. *The Giving Tree*. Harper and Row, 2014.

Discuss *ecosystems* with students and identify the types of ecosystems that exist in your geographical area. Select an ecosystem to study (e.g., forest, meadow, stream, pond). Brainstorm some of the animals and plants that make up that ecosystem and write everything on the board. Have students form a food web by creating links between the items that plants and animals eat and those that eat them.

Assign each student to a particular plant or animal that exists in a specified ecosystem. Have them research (either at the school library or on the internet) what the plant or animal eats, what eats it, and any factors that are necessary in its habitat for survival.

Students will create a note card to identify themselves as a certain plant or animal. All students should start off with a green sticker on their note card, indicating that the population of their plant or animal species is healthy.

Facilitate an exercise in which each person holds hands with the person wearing a sign of the animal or plant that they eat. The result should be a tangled web of students, holding several people's hands.

Now, introduce some human-created scenarios that would affect this eco-system (e.g., an *old-growth forest* is clear-cut, hazardous waste from a factory is dumped into the river, acid rain from factories kills off trees in a forest two hundred miles away). Place a red or black sticker on the person's note card whose animal or plant is affected. For example, pose a scenario where a farmer applies pesticides to the meadow, which kills off the monarch butter-flies. Whoever is playing the role of the monarch butterfly would put a black sticker over top of the green sticker (and should be removed from the web).

Ask students to identify what other species are affected by the disappear-ance of the monarchs in this ecosystem. Place a red sticker over top of the green sticker of those that might be affected, indicating that the species is in trouble (e.g., those that depend on the butterfly for food or serve as prey). Ask students: "What should happen to the ecosystem?"

Repeat the exercise, but this time use examples of recent human actions and efforts to make a positive impact on an ecosystem. For example, tell stu-dents that the fox is reintroduced into an ecosystem and environmental groups helped Congress to pass and enforce laws to protect its habitat.

For an extension, present the class with a scenario that pits human activities against an ecosystem. Break the class into three groups and assign different roles to the different groups. For example, one group could represent a developer that wants to fill in a *wetland* to build a shopping mall, and the other group could represent a group of citizens of that community who want to save the wetland. The third group could represent the new workers who could benefit from jobs at the new mall. Host a debate between the groups.

33. Spinning, Whirling, Dripping[5]

Topics: Weather Measurement

Materials Needed: water, rubbing alcohol, clear narrow-necked bottle, food coloring, 4 clear plastic drinking straws, modeling clay, 5 paper cups, 2 pencils with erasers, hole punch, masking tape, plastic container with lid, paper plate, sand, straight pin, card stock paper, black permanent marker, compass, ruler, glue, two-liter plastic bottle, scissors

Vocabulary:

- Thermometer—an instrument for measuring temperature
- Anemometer—an instrument for measuring the speed of wind
- Wind vane—an instrument used to show the direction of wind
- Rain gauge—an instrument to measure the rain in a given amount of time in an area
- Barometer—an instrument to measure atmospheric pressure

Literature Connections:

Jensen, Belinda. *Spinning Wind and Water: Hurricanes*. Millbrook, 2016.
Rabe, Tish. *Oh Say Can You Say What's the Weather Today? All About the Weather*. Random House Books for Young Readers, 2004.

Pose the question to students: "What kind of instruments are used to measure wind, precipitation, and temperature?" Students can make their own weather instruments with simple materials.

Making a *thermometer*: Inform students that temperature is measured with a thermometer usually made of a glass tube with colored alcohol. As the air gets hotter, the level of the liquid rises and, as the air gets cooler, the level falls. Pour equal amounts of water and alcohol into a bottle and fill to one-fourth of the bottle. Add a couple of drops of food coloring and mix. Put a straw into the bottle, making sure it does not touch the bottom. Use modeling clay to seal the neck of the bottle so the straw stays in place. Have students place their hands on the bottle and observe what happens to the mixture.

Making an *anemometer*: Discuss with students how an anemometer rotates at the same speed as the wind. It gives a direct measure of the speed of the wind. Poke a hole into the side of four cups. Put a straw through two cups to connect them; then do the same thing to the other two cups. Poke a pencil through the fifth cup in the center to make a hole, eraser side down. Balance the cups on the straws across the top of the fifth cup. Make the cups stay on the straws by using masking tape.

Making a *wind vane*: Advise students that knowing the direction of the wind is an important part of predicting weather. The part of the vane that turns into the wind is usually shaped like an arrow, while the other end is wide so that it catches the breeze. The arrow will point to the direction the wind is blowing from. Make the paper plate bottom into a compass rose by writing the directions: north, east, south, and west. Place a blob of clay on the bottom of the plastic container and fill the rest of the way with sand. Snap the lid on and tape it to stay secure. Turn the container upside down and glue onto the paper plate. Poke a pencil through the center of the container so that the eraser is on top and the point is held by the clay. Cut a broad triangle and square about three inches across from the card stock paper. Cut a slit in each end of a straw and slide the triangle into one end and the square into the other. Push the pin through the center of the straw and attach to the eraser. Go outside and use the compass to find the directions to line up the wind vane. Wait for a breeze.

Making a *rain gauge*: Instruct students that rain gauges help farmers manage their crops and prepare for disasters by measuring weather patterns and monitoring floods and droughts. With scissors, cut off the spout top of the two-liter bottle right where the taper or curve begins. Fill the bottom of the bottle with one-half inch of sand. Pour in just enough water so you can see the water level above the sand. Use the marker to mark this "saturation" point above the sand. Place the end of the ruler at the saturation point and draw a line for every inch up to the top of the bottle. Add dots to mark one-fourth, one-half, and three-fourths inch spots between every inch. Take the top part that has been cut off and flip it upside down and fit into the bottle. Secure with masking tape. Place outside in an open area to catch rain.

34. What Poop Is That?[6]

Topic: Identifying Scat
Materials Needed: mixing bowl, spoon, ½ cup hot water, ½ cup coffee grounds, 1⅓ cups flour, 1 cup salt
Vocabulary:

- Scatologist—person who studies wild animal scat
- Scat—excrement of a wild animal; feces; dung

Literature Connections:

Bennett, Artie. *Poopendous!* Blue Apple Books, 2012.

Carlton Books. *Poodunnit: How to Track Animals by Their Poop, Footprints, and More!* Carlton Kids, 2020.

Lehmann, Steph. *Who Pooped? Field Guide, Journal & Activity Book.* Farcountry, 2019.

Robson, Gary D. *Who Pooped in the Park? Yellowstone National Park: Scat and Tracks for Kids.* Farcountry, 2004.

Robson, Gary D. *Who Pooped in the Black Hills? Scat and Tracks for Kids.* Farcountry, 2007.

Examining *scat* is a noninvasive way of studying animal communities. Introduce the term *scatologist*. Scat collection can tell us what animals eat and where they eat, and help us identify animals. Human feces was analyzed by ancient peoples to try to diagnose illnesses. Doctors today often ask about bowel movements when diagnosing illness. The Plains Indians used buffalo dung for fuel. Hunters can identify how close a bear might be by examining scat. The study of scat can begin in the classroom by making mud clay.

Add the hot water to the coffee grounds and stir to dissolve. Add the flour and salt and mix well. Use one of the following web pages to see the different types of animal scat: "Backyard Animal Poop Identification: An Ultimate Guide for 2023" (https://ngpest.com/backyard-animal-poop-identification); "Animal Poop Identification Guide" (https://www.wildliferemoval.com/poop-identification-guide/).

Get students to use the mud clay to form various scat. Place around the room and have students try to identify each other's scat. Once students are familiar with the types of common scat, go for a walk in the woods and see if they can find the real thing. It is very important to note that scat contains many parasites and pathogens that could potentially make you sick. Do not touch scat with your bare hands. Use a stick or gloves to move scat and do not inhale scat scent.

35. Cooking with the Sun[7]

Topic: Solar Oven

Materials Needed: pizza box, aluminum foil, black construction paper, clear plastic wrap, wooden skewers, glue, tape, precision knife, graham crackers, marshmallows, squares of chocolate candy

Vocabulary:

- Solar radiation—light energy from the sun in the form of electromagnetic waves
- Greenhouse effect—warming of the earth's surface and the air above it

Literature Connections:

Alda, Alma Flor. *The Lizard and the Sun*. Dragonfly Books, 1999.

Asch, Frank. *The Sun Is My Favorite Star*. HMH Books for Young Readers, 2008.

Ewing, Clothilde. *Stella Keeps the Sun Up*. Simon & Schuster Books for Young Readers, 2022

Gibbons, Gail. *Sun Up, Sun Down*. HMH Books for Young Readers, 1987.

Kleven, Elisa. *Sun Bread*. Puffin Books, 2004.

Seluk, Nick. *The Sun Is Kind of a Big Deal*. Orchard Books, 2018.

Quiz students: "Where does most of the energy on our planet come from?" Encourage students to research how *solar radiation* can be captured and turned into useful forms of energy. Declare to students that it can get so hot in summer that you might think you could fry an egg on the sidewalk. Ask students: "Do some kinds of surfaces heat up more than others?" "Can you cook food using the sun?" Have students use appendix I as they conduct the experiment.

Use the precision knife to cut a three-sided flap on the top of the pizza box, leaving about one inch between the flap and the sides. Spread glue on the inside of the flap and cover with aluminum foil. Lay black paper on the bottom of the box. Tape layers of clear plastic across the opening under the flap, forming an "oven." Layer a graham cracker, square of chocolate, and marshmallow inside the oven and close the lid with the flap propped open with wooden skewers. Make sure that the sun is shining directly on the oven. Outside temperatures above 85 degrees Fahrenheit is recommended. It can take up to ninety minutes for the s'more to be ready to eat.

Challenge students to describe how the solar oven works: (The oven uses light and heat from the sun to cook the food. The aluminum foil reflects the rays and bounces them into the opening of the box. The heat of the rays is trapped under the plastic wrap and the black paper absorbs the heat.) You may want to vary factors such as the box size, flap size, construction paper color, or outside temperature to encourage students to conduct scientific experiments with the ovens.

Invite students to explore the *greenhouse effect* and determine how it helps the earth (keeps earth from becoming a frozen ball of ice) or hurts the earth (is causing sea levels to rise with melting glaciers). Ask students: "Why have greenhouse gases increased?"

36. We're Going to the Zoo, How about You?

Topic: Zoo Scavenger Hunt
Materials Needed: clipboards, writing tools

Vocabulary:

- Captivity—animals are kept in a place instead of their natural environment
- Adaptation—a change in a trait that helps an organism survive
- Carnivorous—meat-eating organism
- Endangered—in danger of extinction
- Habitat—place that contains the resources an animal needs to survive
- Mammal—warm-blooded animal that feeds its young with milk
- Nocturnal—describes an organism that is active at night
- Amphibian—cold-blooded animal that lives on both land and water

Literature Connections:

Downs, Michael. *You See a Zoo, I See . . .* Charlesbridge, 2022.
Paxton, Tom. *We're Going to the Zoo.* HarperCollins, 1996.

Teaching science through the study of animals can get students to focus on body structure, behaviors, environment, *adaptations*, and strategies that connect to survival skills. Plan a trip to a local zoo. Find out ahead of time if there are any special exhibits during the time of your visit that might connect to science concepts you are currently teaching. Be sure to visit the zoo ahead of time to note what exhibits are closed and any zoo protocols. Prepare students ahead of time on proper behavior and expectations for the field trip. Divide the students into small groups and give each group a clipboard. Some sample questions are included for a scavenger hunt at the zoo:

- Compare the legs of three different animals. How do the legs affect speed? Center of gravity? Which animals need to "push off" to move? In what ways do animals move (e.g., pace, stroll, slither, stomp, prance, gallop, slide, swim)?
- Compare the sounds of three different animals. Which animals have the highest and lowest pitches? Softest and loudest sounds?
- Estimate the height and weight of three different animals. Read the plaques and see how close you were. How does height indicate adaptation to the natural environment of the animal?
- How many *mammals* are in this zoo? Birds? *Amphibians*?
- Do you think it is cruel to put animals in zoos? Why or why not?
- What is the most dangerous animal in this zoo? Why?
- How realistic are the *habitats* for the animals (e.g., arctic temperatures for polar bears)?
- Do you think zoo animals would make good pets? Why or why not?
- Which animals are *nocturnal*? Which animals are *carnivorous*?
- How have the animals in *captivity* adapted from living in the wild?

37. Million-Dollar Property[8]

Topic: Point and Nonpoint Source Pollutants

Materials Needed: long sheet of mural paper, drawing materials, small cut squares of construction paper, personal item from each student (e.g., watch, ring, pencil, hair ribbon)

Vocabulary:

* Point source pollution—identifiable source of contaminant
* Nonpoint source pollution—unidentifiable source of contaminant

Literature Connections:

Cherry, Lynne. *A River Ran Wild: An Environmental History*. HMH Books for Young Readers, 2002.

Dee, Barbara. *Haven Jacobs Saves the Planet*. Aladdin, 2022.

Pego, Ana, and Isabel Minhos Martins. *Plasticus Maritimus: An Invasive Species*. Greystone Kids, 2021.

Simons, Rae. *Pollution Can Make You Sick!* AlphaHouse, 2008.

Apprise students that they have each inherited property along a river and one million dollars to develop the property. Draw a river in the middle of a long sheet of mural paper and divide out properties on each side. Place in the middle of a long table and have students gather around to their assigned property and draw how they would develop their land. Start at the top and have each student describe how they developed their land and how they used water. Then require students to identify any source of pollutants their actions might have caused.

Drop squares of construction paper into the "river" to represent the pollutants. Then have each student drop one personal item into the river. Move the pollutants down the river as each person speaks. After all students have described their development and pollutants, ask the following questions: "How is a student downstream affected by the actions of a student upstream?" "How could students upstream alter the water quality of those downstream?"

Have students reclaim their personal items. Explain that these items represent *point source pollution*. Explain that the squares of construction paper represent *nonpoint source pollution*, as it would be more difficult to claim which squares belonged to which students.

Discuss with students how the quality of water in a river or lake is to a large extent a reflection of the land uses found in its watershed. Review with students the various types of land use: farming, mining, ranching, residential, industrial, recreational. Discuss various ways the types of land use practices might affect the quality of water: disposal of plants and soil causing erosion,

leaks from oil and chemicals, runoff from agricultural fields containing fertil-
izers and pesticides, destabilization of stream channels, disposal of hazardous
waste. You might challenge students to design a community that uses best
management practices that allow for minimum pollutants.

38. Natural Treasures[9]

Topic: Wildlife Scavenger Hunt
Materials Needed: bag for collecting items, camera
Vocabulary:

- Camouflage—disguise to help blend in or appear hidden
- Naturalist—a scientist who studies nature

Literature Connections:

Anderson, Sheila. *What Can Live in a Forest?* Lerner, 2013.
Brremaud, Frederic. *Little Tails in the Forest.* Magnetic, 2017.
Carmichael, L. E. *The Boreal Forest: A Year in the World's Largest Land
    Biome.* Kids Can, 2020.
Dek, Maria. *A Walk in the Forest.* Princeton Architectural, 2017.
Shafer, Sara. *The Bravest Squirrel in the Forest.* Sara Daniel, 2014.

Inform students that today they are going to become *naturalists*. Give students the wildlife scavenger hunt list in appendix J and assign students to go
exploring in a nearby forest or field to see how many items on the list below
they can find. Students can collect the items in a bag or take photographs:

- Partially nibbled acorn
- Animal bone
- Bird feather
- Shell from an animal
- Owl pellet
- Empty cocoon
- Abandoned bird nest
- Animal footprints
- Claw marks on a tree
- Piece of animal fur stuck to thorns
- Snail trail
- Seed pod

Afterward, students will make a list of what animals and insects live
nearby. Discuss how the items on the list help identify organisms in the local

area. Have students indicate how some animals *camouflaged* themselves. Encourage students to make suggestions of other signs of wildlife they could look for on a scavenger hunt.

MORE COMMUNITY AND ENVIRONMENT LITERATURE CONNECTIONS:

Aliki. *My Visit to the Aquarium.* HarperCollins, 1996.
Cronin, Doreen. *Diary of a Worm.* Scholastic, 2004.
Drummond, Allan. *Energy Island: How One Community Harnessed the Wind and Changed Their World.* Square Fish, 2015.
Greenwood, Barbara. *Factory Girl.* Kids Can, 2007.
Guy, Cylita. *Chasing Bats and Tracking Rats: Urban Ecology, Community Science, and How We Share Our Cities.* Annick, 2021.
Hartland, Jessie. *How the Meteorite Got to the Museum.* Blue Apple Books, 2013.
LeFrak, Karen. *Sleepover at the Museum.* Dragonfly Books, 2021.
Mangal, Melina. *Jayden's Impossible Garden.* Free Spirit, 2021.
Messner, Kate. *Up in the Garden and Down in the Dirt.* Chronicle Books, 2017.
Nix, Jackie. *Modern Farms.* Moo Maven, 2021.
Paulsen, Gary. *The Tortilla Factory.* HMH Books for Young Readers, 1998.
Provenson, Alice. *The Year at Maple Hill Farm.* Aladdin, 2001.
Rey, H. A. *Curious George at the Aquarium.* HMH Books for Young Readers, 2014.
Ritchey, Scot. *Look Where We Live! A First Book of Community Building.* Kids Can, 2015.

NOTES

1. Josephine M. Shireen DeSouza, "Nature Teaches: Young Children's Experiences Learning Science Outdoors," in *Science Education Research and Practice in Asia-Pacific and Beyond,* ed. Jennifer Yeo, Tang Wee Teo, and Kok-Sing Tang (Singapore: Springer, 2018), 107–18, https://doi.org/10.1007/978-981-10-5149-4_8.

2. Kim Andrews, *Exploring Nature: Activity Book for Kids* (Emeryville, CA: Rockridge, 2019), x–xi.

3. Southwest Educational Development Laboratory, "Using Community Resources," *Classroom Compass* 3, no. 1 (1996): 1–3, 10.

4. Adapted from lesson "How Many People Does It Take to Ruin an Ecosystem," by Environmental Protection Agency (EPA), *A Teacher's Guide to Reducing, Reusing, and Recycling: The Quest for Less (Activities and Resources for Teaching K–8)* (Washington, DC: Environmental Protection Agency, 2005), 19–21.

5. Adapted from lesson "Designing Your Own Weather Instruments," by Yvette F. Greenspan, *A Guide to Teaching Elementary Science: Ten Easy Steps* (Boston: Sense, 2016), 81–82.

6. Adapted from lesson "Furry Friends," by Andrews, *Exploring Nature*, 76–77.

7. Adapted from lesson "Can You Cook a S'more without Fire or Electricity?," by PBS Learning Media, accessed May 16, 2022, https://static.pbslearningmedia.org/media/media_files/ead1e652-e76b-44f0-b263-1e6b98393763/334b5880-6a04-4b1a-88fb-0f8e93f972b2.pdf.

8. Adapted from lesson "Sum of the Parts," by Western Regional Environmental Education Council, *Project Wet: Curriculum and Activity Guide* (Bozeman, MT: The Watercourse, and Houston, TX: Western Regional Environmental Education Council, 1995), 267–70.

9. Adapted from lesson "Wildlife Scavenger Hunt," by Andrews, *Exploring Nature*, 84–85.

Chapter 6

Using Everyday Objects to Teach Science

Teachers have often used everyday objects to show science principles: dropping eggs down stairwells to show acceleration with gravity, pushing toy cars down ramps to teach Newton's first law of motion, or building paper airplanes to see which designs are more aerodynamic. Thought-provoking science experiments do not have to require elaborate planning or expensive materials. The goal is to encourage students to become more observant, more inquisitive, and highly reflective. School budgets often do not allow the purchase of science materials, so it is beneficial to know ways to use everyday objects to teach science.

One example of using everyday objects as the basis of a scientific experiment is a collection of different types of gloves: thick, woolen gloves; rubber

Illustration by Madalyn Stack.

gloves; leather gloves; silk gloves. Students can test the flexibility, hardness, warmth, and strength of each pair of gloves. Have students try to pick up various objects while wearing the gloves and determine which pair is waterproof. Ask students to explain the usefulness of each pair of gloves and the appropriate time to wear the gloves.[1]

The activities in this chapter allow teachers to use the everyday objects that they have lying around their classroom, schools, or at home to teach science. Teachers are constantly using their own money to enhance the education of their students. Therefore, the science activities in this chapter are designed to show teachers how common and inexpensive materials can be used to teach science concepts. Seeing amazing things happen with common items will open students' eyes to the fact that science is really in everything around them!

The twelve activities in this chapter focus on how to use everyday objects to teach science. Topics covered include: sundials, physical states of water, science with photography, using film to teach science, making paper, freezing point of water, static electricity, air pressure, centripetal force, identifying unknown substances, making fire extinguishers, and surface tension.

ACTIVITIES USING EVERYDAY
OBJECTS TO TEACH SCIENCE

39. Telling Time with Shadows[2]

Topic: Sundials
Materials Needed: 12 small rocks, 12-inch stick, permanent marker, clock
Vocabulary:

- Gnomon—a stick or pillar that casts a shadow of different lengths and directions depending on the sun's position in the sky
- Latitude—the degree north or south of the equator
- True north—direction that points directly to the geographic North Pole
- Hemisphere—one-half of the earth's globe. The equator divides the earth into the Northern and Southern Hemispheres; the prime meridian and the International Date Line divide the earth into the Eastern and Western Hemispheres.
- Solar time—the time on a sundial

Literature Connections:

Anno, Mitsumasa. *Anno's Sundial*. Philomel, 1987.
Koscielniak, Bruce. *About Time: A First Look at Time and Clocks*. Clarion Books, 2013.

Trionfante, Jeffrey V. *Sunclocks: Paper Sundials to Make and Use.* JVT, 1999.

Wells, Robert E. *How Do You Know What Time It Is?* Albert Whitman, 2002.

Ask students: "How did people tell time before there were clocks and watches?" Introduce the sundial—a device that indicates time of day by the position of a shadow. The *gnomon* must be parallel to the axis of the earth's rotation for the sundial to be accurate throughout the year. Sundials need to orient toward *true north*. A sundial at a particular *latitude* in the Northern *Hemisphere* must be reversed for use in the Southern Hemisphere.

Take students outside and choose a place that receives full sun all day. Push the stick into the ground so that it stands securely. For schools in the Northern Hemisphere, angle the stick north at about forty-five degrees, and the opposite for the Southern Hemisphere. Using a clock as a guide, place the rock that corresponds with the time on the shadow line each hour. Check the sundial every hour on the hour. Write the hour on the rock as you place it on the dial. Over twelve hours, the rocks will create a full circle. The sundial will need to be adjusted during daylight saving time, or when the days begin to get shorter or longer.

40. Body Molecules[3]

Topic: Potential and Kinetic Energy

Materials Needed: two flashlights, one covered with a red filter and one with a blue filter

Vocabulary:

- Molecules—smallest units that make up organisms
- Kinetic energy—motion energy
- Potential energy—energy that is stored in an object

Literature Connections:

Bang, Molly, and Penny Chisholm. *Rivers of Sunlight: How the Sun Moves Water around the Earth.* Blue Sky, 2017.

Parker, Bertha Morris. *Matter, Molecules, and Atoms.* Yesterday's Classics, 2018.

Paul, Miranda. *Water Is Water: A Book about the Water Cycle.* Roaring Brook, 2015.

Stein, David Ezra. *Ice Boy.* Candlewick, 2019.

Wells, Robert E. *Did a Dinosaur Drink This Water?* Albert Whitman, 2006.

Discuss with students how water *molecules* are in constant motion. Molecules in warmer water are moving rapidly, while colder water molecules move more slowly. Introduce the ideas of *potential* and *kinetic energy*. Rapid movement causes molecules to bounce off each other, while slow molecules "hang together." Apprise students that today they are going to become water molecules.

First, students will stand in place and move very little to represent molecules in ice with potential energy. Inform students that the flashlight with the red filter represents heat energy to result in increased temperature and molecular motion. Beam the red flashlight on a few students. They begin to slowly move and gently bump into each other. Explain they are now liquid form and should stay close together. Shine the light again to add more heat and turn the liquid to gas.

Students should begin to roam randomly around the room to represent kinetic energy. Inform students that the flashlight with the blue filter represents the loss of heat energy. Shine the blue flashlight on a group of students to return them to liquid. Have students move slower and lose energy as they move together. Continue to shine the blue light until the students act like ice molecules again. Repeat the scenario with various groups of students. For extension activities:

- Provide students with a scenario to act out or write about the actions of the molecules (e.g., a glass of ice set on a sunny porch, a pond from summer to winter).
- Have students create a musical interpretation of molecules in motion.
- Have students create a slideshow presentation or draw illustrations of the various states of water.

41. Picture This: Science

Topic: Science with Photography
Materials Needed: photographs of science concepts, camera phones or iPads, 2 refrigerator boxes, black paint, duct tape, black garbage bags, red gel (from photography store)
Vocabulary:

- Foreground—parts of the scene closest to the photographer
- Background—scene behind the main subject of the photograph
- Composition—how the elements of the photograph are arranged
- Contrast—difference between the lightest and darkest parts of a photograph
- Exposure—amount of light that reaches the film

Literature Connections:

Driscoll, Laura. *Camera: Eureka! The Biography of an Idea*. Astra, 2021.
Jacquart, Anne-Laure. *Photo Adventures for Kids: Solving the Mysteries of Taking Great Photos*. Rocky Nook, 2016.
Loney, Andrea J. *Take a Picture of Me, James Van Der Zee!* Lee & Low Books, 2017.
Martin, Jacqueline Briggs. *Snowflake Bentley*. HMH Books for Young Readers, 2009.

Students are already immersed in photographs and videos through social media, so why not take advantage of their interest and connect it to science? Introduce the photography vocabulary to students. Students will create a digital science notebook to document their experiments. Examples include: use time-lapse photography to show growth of a plant or slow motion to show movement, have an outdoor scavenger hunt for plants and animals, take photographs that represent the water cycle, or take pictures through telescopes and microscopes to share with the whole group.[4]

One activity you can do with students is to show photographs focused on habitats. After allowing time for observations, pose the following questions to students:

- In what part of the world might you find this habitat?
- What animals might live in this habitat?
- What range of temperatures might you find?
- What inferences can you make from the pictures?

Teach students about the science of photography: How do cameras work? How is light important to photography? How is chemistry used in photography? A good web page to use is "The (Basic) Science behind Photography" at https://crimsonnews.org/2727/entertainment/the-basic-science-behind-photography/.

Students can build their own darkroom with two refrigerator boxes. Paint the interior black and tape the boxes together. Near the top, cut a small hole and cover it with red gel to allow a small amount of "safe" light into the darkroom. Cut a hole in the side of the box for a door and hang black garbage bags over it to keep the room dark.[5] Invite a local photographer to speak to the class and demonstrate how to develop pictures.

42. Lights! Action! Science!

Topic: Science in Film
Materials Needed: access to a streaming service to show films

Vocabulary:

- B movie—a low-budget movie
- Genre—a style of movie, book, music, and so on
- Cosmos—the universe
- Interstellar—occurring among the stars
- Terraforming—modifying a planet so that it is similar to Earth in order to make it habitable for humans

Literature Connections:

Brake, Mark. *The Super Cool Science of Star Wars: The Saber-Swirling Science behind the Death Star, Aliens, and Life in That Galaxy Far, Far Away!* Sky Pony, 2020.

Loh-Hagan, Virginia. *Weird Science Movies (How the Heck Does That Work?!).* 45th Parallel, 2021.

Perritano, John. *The Science of Movies.* Turtleback, 2017.

Science fiction films show us possible worlds, futuristic life, and technological progress, and often touch on social and ethical issues. These films give us ideas about how to make a better world for future generations. Many of our fears show up in science fiction films: medical scientists modifying genes, artificial intelligence (AI) beings taking control, "Big Brother" watching everything we do. As with science fiction books, teachers need to remind students that these films are still fiction. Students can watch the movies, then conduct research to find facts to support or dispute events in the films. Below is a list of science fiction films that teachers can use to teach science:

- *The Andromeda Strain* (directed by Robert Wise; Universal Pictures, 1971)—a team of scientists investigate a deadly organism of extraterrestrial origin that killed citizens of a small town and race to find a cure.
- *Hidden Figures* (directed by Theodore Melfi; Fox 2000 Pictures, Chernin Entertainment and Levitine Films, 2016)—the story of African American female mathematicians who served vital roles at NASA during the early years of the space program.
- *Apollo 13* (directed by Ron Howard; Universal Pictures and Imagine Entertainment, 1995)—when an on-board explosion of the spaceship causes internal damage, NASA personnel must seek scientific and mechanical solutions to get the men home safely.
- *October Sky* (directed by Joe Johnston; Universal Pictures, 1999)—true story of Homer Hickman, a coal miner's son, who was inspired by the Sputnik launch to go on to become a NASA engineer.

- *The Manhattan Project* (directed by Marshall Brickman; Gladden Entertainment, 1986)—a gifted high school student steals a container of plutonium to build an atomic bomb for a national science fair and expose a nuclear weapons lab.
- *The Martian* (directed by Ridley Scott; Scott Free Productions, Kinberg Genre, and TSG Entertainment, 2015)—a lone astronaut stranded on Mars struggles to survive while his team attempts to return and rescue him.
- *The Right Stuff* (directed by Phillip Kaufman; Ladd Company, 1983)—follows test pilots who work with the space program to break the sound barrier and help prepare for the selection of the Mercury 7 astronauts.

Other films can also be used to introduce various science concepts. *The Lego Movie* (directed by Phil Lord and Christopher Miller; Warner Animation Group, 2014) shows creative engineering solutions; *Big Hero 6* (directed by Don Hall and Chris Williams; Walt Disney Pictures, 2014) follows a robotics prodigy who develops microbots; *Underwater Dreams* (directed by Mary Mazzio; 50 Eggs Film, 2014) follows a high school team that participates in an underwater robotics competition; and *The Imitation Game* (directed by Morten Tyldum; Black Bear Pictures, 2014) dramatizes cryptologists and mathematicians attempting to crack the German Enigma code during World War II.

Neil deGrasse Tyson, well-known astrophysicist, often posts tweets after watching movies and comments on the science issues (@neiltyson). Jacob Clark Blickenstaff, with the National Science Teachers of America, hosts a movie blog to help teachers sort the good and bad science of movies (https://www.nsta.org/blick-flicks). Have students become movie critics and tweet their own responses to the movies they watch. Encourage students to find examples of science fiction films with *interstellar* themes or ones that portray *terraforming* or the *cosmos*. Ask students to determine if the films are *B movies* or box office hits.

43. Pulp and Paper

Topic: Making Paper

Materials Needed: various types of paper (tissue, foil, tracing, construction, wrapping), tagboard, glue, staplers, scissors, tape, paper clips, blender, scraps of paper (junk mail, newspaper, wrapping paper, old letters or notes), water, plastic tub, 8x10 wooden picture frame, piece of screen a little bigger than picture frame with small holes, sponge, 2 folded towels, drawing tools, large brown paper bags

Vocabulary:

- Opaque—not able to see through
- Transparent—easy to see through
- Cellulose—threads of fiber found in the walls of green plants that can be used to make paper
- Recycle—use something old to make something new

Literature Connections:

Aerts, Jef. *Cherry Blossom and Paper Planes*. Floris Books, 2020.
Daywalt, Drew. *The Legend of Rock Paper Scissors*. Balzer & Bray, 2017.
Jeffers, Oliver. *The Great Paper Caper*. Philomel Books, 2009.
Rhee, Helena Ku. *The Paper Kingdom*. Random House Books for Young Readers, 2020.

Create a discovery table for exploring paper by laying out different types of papers: tissue, foil, tracing paper, construction paper, tagboard, wrapping paper. Encourage children to use their hands, eyes, and ears to explore the paper. Have students label papers using terms: smooth, rough, shiny, *transparent*, *opaque*, thin, thick, rectangular, heavy, light. Provide students with glue, staplers, paper clips, scissors, and tape, and let students explore what they can do with paper (fold, cut, tear, shape).[6]

Discuss with students how early writing material was made from the papyrus plant. Other early types of writing materials around the world include bamboo, silk, shells, metal, clay, wood, tree bark, stone, skins of fishes, animal hides, and bones. Paper was made in China from rags and fibers repeatedly soaked, pounded, bleached, washed, and strained. The mush was then dried in a mesh frame. Paper today is made from wood chips mixed with chemicals and pressure-boiled to make pulp. Most papers are assemblies of fibers of *cellulose*.

Students can make their own paper from *recycled* scrap papers. Fill a blender jar half full with torn paper scraps. Fill the rest of the jar with water and put the lid on. Blend for one or two minutes until the paper pieces are chopped into a pulp. Pour the pulp into the plastic tub, refill the blender jar with warm water, and pour into the tub. Mix it all together with your hands. Staple the screen onto the 8x10 frame.

Dip the frame into the tub, cover with pulp, and spread evenly over the screen. Pull the frame straight up and shake gently to remove extra water. Use the sponge to soak up water under the screen. Set the frame on a folded towel; then press another towel on top of the paper. Carefully peel the paper off and lay the towel with the sheet of paper on it flat on a counter to dry.[7]

Tell students that in many parts of the world the prepared skins of animals were used to make a writing material called parchment. Parchment was a heavier and more durable writing material than papyrus and could be washed or scraped off and reused. Give students a large brown paper bag and ask them to tear it out flat, then cut out a smaller portion of the paper to resemble a buffalo skin. Crumple the paper and open it several times to create a smooth, parchment-like surface.

Have students draw any type of script or pictorial representation on their parchment. Discussions about the use of buffalo skins by Native Americans and cattle skins by other peoples can lead to the conclusion that parchment would not have been used in India, Southeast Asia, or East Asia because the use of butchered animal skins to write sacred texts offended the religious beliefs of Hindus and Buddhists.

44. Salt and Water

Topic: Freezing Point of Water
Materials Needed: ice cubes, glasses, cold water, strings cut into 4-inch lengths, salt, sugar, half-and-half, vanilla extract, large and small ziplock bags, spoons, gloves
Vocabulary:

- Celsius—unit of temperature based on 0 degrees as the freezing point of water and 100 degrees as the boiling point of water
- Fahrenheit—unit of temperature based on 32 degrees as the freezing point of water and 212 degrees as the boiling point of water
- Adhere—stick fast to
- Ions—atoms that bear positive or negative electric charges

Literature Connections:

Bader, Bonnie. *Curious about Ice Cream*. Penguin Young Readers, 2017.
Gibbons, Gail. *Ice Cream: The Full Scoop*. Holiday House, 2008.
Kheiriyeh, Rashin. *Saffron Ice Cream*. Arthur A. Levine Books, 2018.
Mason, Adrienne. *Change It! Solids, Liquids, Gases and You*. Kids Can, 2006.
Stein, David Ezra. *Ice Boy*. Candlewick, 2019.
Yuh, Joanne. *Meet the H2O Family*. No publisher, 2019.

Inquire of students: "Why is salt used in winter to deice roads?" Provide further information of how water temperature is a result of how fast or slow the water molecules move. At 0 degrees *Celsius* (32 degrees *Fahrenheit*), the molecules form strong connections and water freezes. When water is not pure (contains sugar or salt), the temperature at which it turns solid is lower than 0 degrees Celsius. Salt on roads in winter lowers the freezing point of water.

Salt is made of two *ions*: sodium (which is positively charged) and chloride (which is negatively charged). When salt is added to other polar molecules such as water, the salt ions break apart and *adhere* to their corresponding oppositely charged part of the water molecules. This disrupts the hydrogen bonding between water molecules, thus lowering the freezing point of water.

Challenge students to lift an ice cube out of a glass of water using only a string, no fingers. After a few minutes of trying, have the students lay the string across a cube floating near the top of the glass and sprinkle salt on the cube and string. Leave for a few minutes; then lift the string. The cube should have melted into the string. Challenge the students to use sugar and see if the results are the same.

Of course, the best way to demonstrate lowering the freezing point of water is to make ice cream. Pour 1 cup of half-and-half into a small ziplock bag. Add 1½ teaspoons vanilla extract and 1 tablespoon sugar. Seal the bag firmly. In a larger ziplock bag, fill with ice halfway; then add ¼ cup of salt (the more salt you add, the lower the freezing point becomes). Place the small bag inside the large bag and fill with ice to the top. Seal the large bag; then shake for about fifteen minutes. You will want to wear gloves, as the salt makes the ice very cold. Take the small bag out and rinse well with water to remove any salt. Open the bag, mix around with a spoon, and then scoop out and eat.[8]

45. All Charged Up[9]

Topic: Static Electricity

Materials Needed: plastic rods, pieces of cloth, balloons, salt, pepper, plates, cans, rulers, combs, markers, tissue paper, plastic bags, plastic spoons, table tennis balls, packing peanuts, types of paper

Vocabulary:

- Levitate—rise or float in the air
- Electron—particle with a negative charge
- Proton—particle with a positive charge
- Static electricity—results from imbalance of electrons in objects

Literature Connections:

Boothroyd, Jennifer. *All Charged Up: A Look at Electricity*. Lerner, 2019.
Davis, Jermey. *Tutu and the Science Crew: Static Electricity*. Independently published, 2018.
Dongni, Bao. *Matilda Experiences Static Electricity*. WS Education, 2021.

Knowlton-Thorne, Michele. *Picture Day Pandemonium*. Know It All
Books, 2020.

Ask students: "Have you ever felt a shock when you touched something?"
"What causes this?" Discuss with students how all matter is made up of
atoms, which are made of positive (*protons*) and negative (*electrons*) particles.
When you rub two things together, some electrons move to one of the items.
Too many electrons cause an item to be negatively charged, and not enough
electrons causes a positive charge. The imbalance of charges is called *static
electricity*. Opposite charges will attract to each other, just as with a magnet.

There are many fun activities you can do with static electricity in the
classroom:

- Give students a variety of materials (e.g., ruler, comb, marker) and have
  them rub them together to build up a static charge. Bring the charged
  object near lightweight materials (e.g., balloons, packing peanuts, table
  tennis ball) and see which materials work best at holding an object.
- *Levitate* a plastic bag by rubbing the surface of a plastic rod with a piece
  of cloth for forty seconds, then rubbing the plastic bag with the cloth for
  forty seconds. The rod and cloth become negatively charged and repel
  each other, causing the bag to levitate as you wave the rod below.
- Rub the surface of a plastic rod with a piece of cloth for forty seconds.
  Hold the rod close to a can (placed on its side) without touching it and
  watch as it follows the movement of the rod. The negative charge of the
  rod reacts to the positive charge of the can, and the attraction causes the
  can to roll toward the rod.
- Mix salt and pepper together on a plate and ask students how they might
  separate the two ingredients. Rub a plastic spoon with a cloth for forty
  seconds. Hold the spoon over the mixture and watch the pepper jump up
  and stick to the spoon. Because pepper is lighter than salt, it will jump
  more easily and stick to the spoon.
- Cut lightweight paper into frog shapes. Blow up a balloon and rub it
  on your hair. Hold the balloon above the frogs and watch them jump.
  Experiment with different weights of paper and different-sized frog
  shapes. See who can make their frog stick to the balloon the longest.[10]

46. Can You Take the Pressure?

Topic: Air Pressure
Materials Needed: straws, plastic cups, water, pushpins, bucket of ice
  water, empty soda can, hot plate, tongs, potato, hard-boiled egg,

matches, glass milk bottle, jar, small votive candle, shallow dish, blue food coloring

Vocabulary:

- Air pressure—force exerted by air pushing on an area
- Barometer—instrument used to measure air pressure
- Atmosphere—envelope of gases that surround the earth

Literature Connections:

Branley, Franklyn M. *Air Is All around You*. HarperCollins, 2006.
Edom, Helen, and Moira Butterfield. *Science with Air*. Usborne, 2008.
Gibbons, Gail. *Weather Words and What They Mean*. Holiday House, 2019.
Lerbinger, Otto. *Air*. B.E.S., 1995.

Question students: "How does a straw work?" Discuss how the *atmosphere* is pushing down on us, while the gas inside our bodies is pushing back so we don't get crushed. Assign students to fill a plastic cup about halfway with water and place a straw in the cup. Ask students to predict what will happen when they place their finger over the top of the straw and lift it out of the water. Have them remove their finger and watch the water fall back into the cup. Question students as to why this happens.

Explain that the atmosphere pushes the liquid in the glass up into the straw. When a finger covers the top hole of the straw, a difference in *air pressure* below the straw is holding the water in place. Using a pushpin, poke a hole in the straw about two centimeters from the top. Place the straw in the water again and ask students to predict what will happen when they place a finger over the top and lift the straw out of the water. Have them remove their finger and observe. Explain that when air can enter the straw through the hole, the air pressure cannot support the water in the straw.

Instruct students to get a new straw and place it in the cup of water and take a sip. When you suck through a straw, you take the atmosphere out of the straw. Remove the straw and poke a hole about two centimeters from the top of the straw. Place in the cup again and try to sip. When you suck on a straw that has a hole in the side, you pull air through the hole, instead of removing air. Have students explain in their own words how air pressure is at work.[11] Discuss with students how low pressure is generally associated with bad weather and high pressure with good weather. Air pressure is measured with a *barometer*.

There are many other ways to show the effects of air pressure. Fill an empty soda can with one centimeter of water. Place on the hot plate until the water boils. Using the tongs, remove the can and quickly invert it and submerge into the bucket of ice water. The can will crush because the air pressure on the inside becomes less than the pressure on the outside.[12]

Hold a potato in one hand and a straw in the other hand. Place your forefinger over the top opening of the straw. Strike the potato quickly with a lot of force, keeping the straw perpendicular to the surface of the potato. You should be able to puncture the potato with the straw.[13]

Remove the shell from a hard-boiled egg. Drop a burning match into a glass milk bottle; then stand the egg on the mouth of the bottle. When the flame goes out, the air inside the bottle will contract, form a vacuum, and pull the egg inside. Turn the bottle upside down so the egg falls into the neck. Tip back your head and blow into the bottle mouth. When you remove your mouth, the egg will pop out.[14]

Fill the shallow dish with water and add blue food coloring. Place the candle in the middle of the dish and light it. Quickly place the empty jar over the flame, touching the water. When the candle burns out, the water will rise up into the jar. This experiment illustrates Charles's law, which states that the volume of gas is proportionate to the absolute temperature of gas at constant pressure.[15] Other examples include tires deflating in cold temperatures, or a pool float bursting in the hot sun when overinflated.

47. Penny for Your Force[16]

Topic: Centripetal Force
Materials Needed: wire hanger, penny
Vocabulary:

- Force—push or pull
- Centripetal force—keeps objects moving in a curved or circular path
- Centrifugal force—tendency of an object moving in a circle to travel away from the center
- Tether—a rope or chain used to restrain an object
- Inertia—resistance of a body to a change in its speed or direction of motion

Literature Connections:

Amin, Anita Nahta. *Force and Motion (Foundations of Physics)*. Pogo, 2021.
Boothroyd, Jennifer. *Give It a Push! Give It a Pull: A Look at Forces*. LernerClassroom, 2010.
Bradley, Kimberly. *Forces Make Things Move*. HarperCollins, 2005.
Pettiford, Rebecca. *Roller Coasters (Amazing Structures)*. Jump!, 2016.
Weakland, Mark Andrew. *When Amelia Earhart Built a Roller Coaster*. Picture Window Books, 2016.

Ask students: "Why you don't fall out of an upside-down loop on a roller coaster?" "How can a satellite stay in orbit around the earth?" Discuss that there are many different *forces* in the universe. With *centripetal force*, an object moves in a circular path. The game *tether* ball uses a string to attach a ball to a pole and keep the ball in a circular motion. Ask students: "Can a tether ball demonstrate *inertia*?" (a ball with more mass will have more inertia, needing a greater force to accelerate it).

A yo-yo is another example of an object that moves in a circle due to centripetal force. The sun's gravity keeps planets moving in its orbit. Medical personnel use centripetal force to separate red blood cells from plasma. The opposite of centripetal force is *centrifugal force*, which causes a body to fly away from the center.

Bend the hook portion of the wire hanger to create a level surface. Stretch the hanger into the shape of a diamond. Balance the penny on the hooked end of the hanger and swing back and forth. Gradually increase the swing until you can spin it in a full circle. Explain to students that objects that move in a circle experience centripetal force. According to Newton's first law of motion, objects remain in motion unless acted upon by an external force. Ask students: "What will happen if you swing the hanger too slowly? Why?"

48. Mystery Powder[17]

Topic: Identifying Unknown Substances

Materials Needed: baking soda, cornstarch, granular sugar, baking powder, powdered sugar, small plastic bags, colored markers, eyedroppers, bottle of iodine for each group, 5 popsicle sticks for each group, 5 paper plates for each group, water, vinegar

Vocabulary:

- Solubility—capability of being dissolved
- Physical property—characteristic of matter that can be observed or measured
- Chemical property—characteristic that can be observed when a substance undergoes chemical change

Literature Connections:

Adams, Tom. *Super Science: Matter Matters!* Templar, 2012.
Braun, Eric. *Joe-Joe the Wizard Brews Up Solids, Liquids, and Gases.* Picture Window Books. 2014.
Kjelle, Marylou Morano. *The Properties of Salt.* Powerkids, 2006.
Ross, Michael Elsohn. *What's the Matter in Mr. Whiskers' Room?* Candlewick, 2007.

Tell students that they are working in a crime lab and have been given five different white powders from the scene of a crime. Their mission is to identify each powder. These powders are in color-coded bags. Place each of the powders in a plastic bag and label with markers as red, green, blue, yellow, and orange. Color the tips of each popsicle stick as one of the colors. Ask students to discuss ways that they could identify *physical* or *chemical properties* of each of the powders (observation, smell, taste, touch, *solubility*). Place the students into small groups. Have each group complete the Mystery Powder Table in appendix K as they experiment with each powder.

First, have students observe the powders and guess what each might be. Next, have students touch, then smell each powder and guess what it might be. Then, have students scoop out a small portion of the powder onto a popsicle stick (e.g., red stick scoops out of the red bag), place on a paper plate, and use an eyedropper to drop water onto the powder and stir. Ask students to identify what happens with each powder. Do the same with vinegar, then iodine. Based on their evidence, have students identify each powder.

49. Foam Alone[18]

Topic: Making a Fire Extinguisher
Materials Needed: baking soda, vinegar, empty plastic soda bottle, tissue, rubber band
Vocabulary:

• Extinguish—cause a fire to cease to burn
• Retardant—a substance that prevents fire from growing or spreading

Literature Connections:

Ashman, Linda. *Fire Chief Fran*. Astra Young Readers, 2022.
Gibbons, Gail. *Fire! Fire!* HarperCollins, 1987.
Harper, Jamie. *Miss Mingo and the Fire Drill*. Candlewick, 2012.

Students can make a portable fire extinguisher using a few household materials. Fill a soda bottle halfway with vinegar. Form the tissue into a cup shape and poke it into the mouth of the bottle, leaving the sides of the tissue over the rim of the bottle. Pour baking soda into the tissue, then place a rubber band around the bottle opening over the tissue to keep it from dropping into the bottle. Replace the cap on the bottle while it is in storage. When ready to use, shake the bottle vigorously and remove the cap. The fire-*retardant* foam that forms can be poured over a fire to *extinguish* the flames.

Ask students: "Is this a chemical or physical reaction?" (In this experiment, carbon dioxide is produced, which is a chemical reaction.) Fire needs oxygen and fuel to burn. Taking away either causes the fire to go out.

50. Water Drops on a Penny[19]

Topic: Surface Tension
Materials Needed: pennies (1 per student or group), medicine droppers or eyedroppers, cups, tap water, dish soap, paper towels
Vocabulary:

- Hypothesis—educated guess, based on information you already know
- Surface tension—a force that causes a layer of liquid to behave like an elastic sheet or skin; the property of the surface of a liquid that allows it to resist an external force, due to the cohesive nature of its molecules
- Variable—characteristic or condition that exists in different amounts or types and can be changed in an experiment

Literature Connections:

Andros, Camille. *Charlotte the Scientist Is Squished.* Clarion Books, 2017.
Baby Professor. *What Is the Scientific Method? Science Book for Kids.* Baby Professor, 2017.
Braun, Eric Mark. *Mad Margaret Experiments with the Scientific Method.* Picture Window Books, 2012.
Offill, Jenny. *11 Experiments That Failed.* Schwartz & Wade, 2011.

Review the definition of *hypothesis.* Tell students that good scientists come up with a hypothesis before they start an experiment. In fact, it is part of the scientific method. Remind students of the steps of the scientific method: make an observation, ask a question, form a hypothesis, design an experiment, conduct an experiment, draw conclusions, report results, and optionally repeat the experiment.

Hand out a penny to each student or to small groups of students. Have students make observations about the surface of the penny and record them on their data sheets (see appendix L). Introduce the problem question: "How many water drops can fit on the surface of a penny?" Have students write down their hypothesis on the data sheet. Remind students that they are not to change their hypothesis during the experiment. Tell students that scientists know that their hypothesis may not be accurate and that good scientists learn from their incorrect guesses. After all students have made their hypothesis, it is time to start the experiment.

Lay each penny on a paper towel on a flat surface. Have students use the dropper to add water drop by drop to the surface of the penny. As students add water, have them record tallies on their data sheet. Tell students to hold the dropper slightly over the penny (not touching it) so each new drop has to fall a short distance before merging with the water on the penny. Students should continue to add drops (refilling the dropper as needed) until the first drop spills over the edge of the penny.

Have students use a paper towel to clean off the penny and any water on their work surface. Once all students/groups finish the experiment, discuss as a group how many drops fit on the surface of the penny. Ask students to reflect on their hypothesis. Did anyone guess the exact number? Was anyone even close? Ask students why the penny's small surface area was able to fit so many drops of water. Introduce the vocabulary term *surface tension*.

Set up the next experiment with only one *variable* changing: using dish soap water instead of tap water. Have students make a new hypothesis using the knowledge they gained from the first experiment, but taking into account the changing variable. Have students conduct the experiment as before, keeping tallies and ending it when the first drop spills over the edge. After all groups have finished with the second trial, discuss again the results and possible reasons for the difference in the two experiments.

Students should find that the tap water produces a larger, stable drop of water. The reason behind this is that the plain tap water has a higher surface tension. This makes the surface of the drop stronger and is therefore able to hold together a bigger drop. When soap is added to the water, it lowers the water's surface tension. The drop becomes weaker and breaks apart sooner than the plain tap water. Discuss with students that this characteristic is actually what makes dish soap useful. Making water molecules stick together less allows soap to clean dishes more easily. On the data sheet, have students identify other liquids they could try and predict the results.

NOTES

1. Antonella Bachiorri, Paola Bortolon, Maria Angela Fontechiari, Frankie McKeon, and Anna Pascucci, *Everyday Objects: Linking IBSE and ESD* (UK: Lifelong Learning Programme of the European Union, 2016), accessed May 18, 2022, https://fondation-lamap.org/sites/default/files/upload/media/minisites/sustain/Everyday_objects_handbook.pdf; accessed May 18, 2022, http://www.pef.unilj.si/fileadmin/Datoteke/Projekti/SUSTAIN/Everyday_objects_handbook.pdf.

2. Adapted from lesson "Around the Clock," by Kim Andrews, *Exploring Nature: Activity Book for Kids* (Emeryville, CA: Rockridge, 2019), 38–39.

3. Adapted from lesson "Molecules in Motion," by Western Regional Environmental Education Council, *Project Wet: Curriculum and Activity Guide* (Bozeman, MT: The Watercourse, and Houston, TX: Western Regional Environmental Education Council, 1995), 47–49.

4. Karen Sinai, "13 Ways Photography Helps You Teach Science," *Science by Sinai: Middle School Science Tips, Ideas, and Resources* (blog), December 12, 2021, https://sciencebysinai.com/ways-using-photography-helps-you-teach-science/.

5. Hilary Masell Oswald, "Picture This: Using Photography to Teach Science, Math, and Writing," George Lucas Education Foundation: Edutopia, July 30, 2008, https://www.edutopia.org/photography-how-to-project-learning.

6. Carol Seefeldt, "Teaching Science through the Visual Arts and Music," *Scholastic Early Childhood Today* 18, no. 6 (2004): 29–34.

7. Adapted from lesson "How to Make Paper," *HST Resource Center* (blog), accessed May 2, 2022, https://learning-center.homesciencetools.com/article/how-to-make-paper-science-project-for-elementary/.

8. Adapted from lesson "Ice Cream in a Bag," by Kimberly McLeod, *The Best Ideas for Kids* (blog), April 30, 2021, https://www.thebestideasforkids.com/ice-cream-in-a-bag/.

9. Adapted from lesson "5 Easy Static Electricity Experiments," by Rachel, *Titus 2 Homemaker* (blog), January 9, 2017, https://titus2homemaker.com/5-easy-static-electricity-experiments-do-try-this-at-home/.

10. Adapted from lesson "Jumping Frogs—A Static Electricity Experiment," by Emma Vanstone, *Science Sparks* (blog), May 2, 2019, https://www.science-sparks.com/jumping-frogs/.

11. Adapted from lesson, "Straws and Air Pressure: Using an Everyday Object to Explain Air Pressure," by Deborah McCarthy, *Science Scope* 37 no. 8 (2014): 23–28.

12. Adapted from lesson "Air Pressure Experiments: I Can't Take the Pressure!," *Teach Engineering* (blog), accessed May 4, 2022, from https://www.teachengineering.org/activities/view/cub_air_lesson04_activity1.

13. Adapted from lesson "Potato Puncture," by Martin Gardner, *Entertaining Science Experiments with Everyday Objects* (New York: Dover, 1981), 99.

14. Gardner, *Entertaining Science Experiments*.

15. Adapted from lesson "Rising Water Experiment," *Team Cartwright* (blog), December 8, 2021, https://team-cartwright.com/rising-water-experiment/.

16. Adapted from lesson "Centripetal Force Penny," by Steve Spangler, *10-Minute Science Experiments* (New York: Topix Media Lab 2019), 66–67.

17. Adapted from lesson "Mystery Powder," by Yvette F. Greenspan, *A Guide to Teaching Elementary Science: Ten Easy Steps* (Boston: Sense, 2016), 97–99.

18. Adapted from lesson "Foam Alone: Make a Sneaky Fire Extinguisher," by Cy Tymony, *Sneaky Uses for Everyday Things* (Kansas City, MO: Andrews McMeel, 2020), 59–60.

19. Adapted from lesson "Measure Surface Tension with a Penny," Science Buddies, *Scientific American*, June 25, 2015, https://www.scientificamerican.com/article/measure-surface-tension-with-a-penny/.

Conclusion

Young children are naturally curious about the world around them. From birth, children observe, explore, ask questions, and experiment. Teaching science to students helps them increase their understanding of how and why things work, and make sense of the world around them. Through the trial and error of experimentation, students learn that if something does not work the first time, try it again. Students learn that following instructions and communicating results is important. Training young scientists instills the ability to think logically and solve problems, ask questions, collect information, test ideas, and apply what was learned.

Students in classes can vary hugely in terms of interest in science, prior knowledge, and ability to use the scientific method of learning and thinking. By focusing on the scientific process of discovery, more students will be engaged and interested in learning science. The teaching of science needs to be much more than memorizing theories, formulas, or vocabulary. Science is the study of the world through observation and experimentation.

There has been a push in recent years toward a STEAM education (science, technology, engineering, art, mathematics). Integrating science is the key to innovation, global competitiveness, availability of energy and resources, management of health and well-being, water quality, waste management, and human advancement. It is imperative that teachers create opportunities for students to apply science using everyday materials and not only reading about it in a textbook. This connects science to the real world.

Science is everywhere. It is in infrastructure designed by civil engineers and planners, in trees that create the oxygen we need to survive, in communication devices, transportation devices, and all forms of energy. Careers in medicine, engineering, and environmental work use a strong foundation of science. With this book in hand, teachers can inspire new scientists to take on world problems and save the future.

Resources

This part of the book includes templates and ideas that could be used along with the activities from the book, with activities you already use in your science class, or with different concepts you teach throughout the year. The resources are divided into four sections: "Templates to Use before Activities," "Templates to Use during Activities," "Templates to Use after Activities," and "Vocabulary Activities." For busy teachers, these resources will be valuable and available for quick and easy use.

Activating students' prior knowledge and setting the stage for investigations is a great way for teachers to grab students' attention from the start. Good scientists do not jump into experiments without thinking about possible and probable outcomes. The "Templates to Use before Activities" can be used prior to starting an activity to encourage students to engage in the scientific method, make predictions, and activate prior knowledge.

Even while students are engaged in high-level science activities, it is important to get a glimpse into their thinking and get them to practice record keeping. Scientists have to make observations during an experiment to fully investigate what is happening, explain why it happened, make adjustments for future experiments, and be prepared to share their findings with others in the scientific community. The templates in the "Templates to Use during Activities" section are designed to facilitate students' record keeping during activities in the science classroom.

Many students love science because they equate it with hands-on experiments. However, teachers know that conducting experiments without reflection on the how and why is not an effective way to teach science concepts. The "Templates to Use after Activities" section gives templates designed to have students reflect on activities that they do in science after the activity is over. Students will be required to use the data collected during the activity and science concepts to synthesize their information.

Finally, the last section includes ideas to reinforce and review vocabulary. Most of the ideas are based on games with which teachers and students are already familiar. Science, like most school subjects, has a language all its own. Teachers know that students need exposure to curricular vocabulary and students must learn what the terms mean in order to master science concepts, think like a scientist, and explain the world around them. The ideas and templates in this section can be applied to any set of vocabulary terms. They can be used as an introduction, instruction, or review for the lesson.

TEMPLATES TO USE BEFORE ACTIVITIES

A. Scientific Method Recording Sheet
B. Making Predictions Chart
C. Anticipation Chart

A. Scientific Method Recording Sheet

Make an observation. (What do you notice about the world around you?)

_____

_____

Ask a question. (What do you wonder? What would you like to find out?)

_____

_____

Form a hypothesis. (What do you think will happen? What will be the outcome?)

_____

_____

Design an experiment. Think about what supplies will be needed. (What will it look like? What conditions will be applied? Do you have a control group?)

Describe	*Illustrate*

Draw conclusions. (What happened in the experiment? How can you explain the results? Check your hypothesis.)

Share your results with someone! Repeat the experiment if needed with new conditions.

B. Making Predictions Chart

Prediction *What do you think will happen?*	*Reasoning* *Why do you think that will happen?*

Was your prediction correct? _____yes _____no

What ended up happening?

_____

_____

_____

Why do you think it happened that way?

_____

_____

_____

C. Anticipation Chart*

Topic or Idea:		
What do you think you know about the topic or idea?	What facts do you want to learn about this topic or idea?	How do you want to learn about this topic or idea? (e.g., group, partner, individual, videos, reading, lecture, games, music, art)

*Adapted from ideas by J. L. Roberts and J. R. Boggess, *Teacher's Survival Guide: Gifted Education* (Waco, TX: Prufrock, 2011), 105.

TEMPLATES TO USE DURING ACTIVITIES

A. Knew-New Chart
B. Shape Notes Template
C. 1-2-3-4 Template

A. Knew-New Chart

KNEW	NEW
Information I already knew	**Information I learned**

B. Shape Notes Template

Write notes, words, and ideas in the shapes from our work in class today.

C. 1-2-3-4 Template

Use the template to evaluate your experiment.

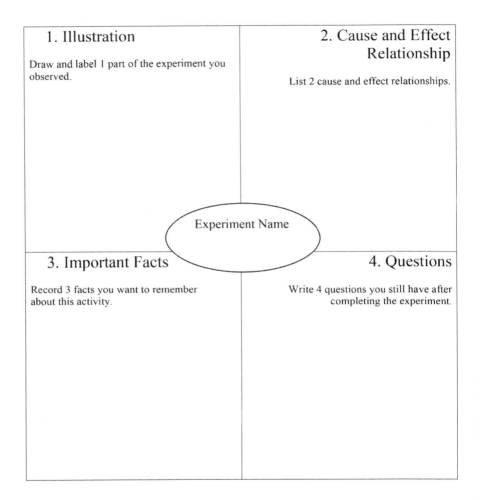

TEMPLATES TO USE AFTER ACTIVITIES

A. Rubric for Experiments
B. Choice Board
C. Claim, Evidence, Reasoning (CER) Chart

A. Rubric for Experiments

	Advanced Scientist 3	*Scientist* 2	*Beginning Scientist* 1
Question/ Hypothesis	Question and hypothesis are stated clearly and are testable.	Question and hypothesis are stated, and are somewhat clear and testable.	Question is not clear and testable; hypothesis is not clear.
Research	Research is thorough, specific, and includes three or more examples.	Research is thorough and includes at least two examples.	Research is minimal and one or no examples are included.
Experiment Design/ Procedures/ Materials	Experiment design, procedures, and materials are organized and easy to follow.	Experiment design, procedures, and materials are organized and somewhat easy to follow.	Experiment design, procedures, and materials are not organized and are difficult to follow.
Results	Data is presented and relates to the question/ hypothesis.	Data is presented and somewhat relates to the question/ hypothesis.	Data is presented but is not related to the question/hypothesis.
Conclusion	The conclusion is supported by the data collected.	The conclusion is somewhat supported by the data collected.	The conclusion is not supported by the data collected.

B. Choice Board

The following questions can be asked after any experiment to check for understanding:

How were you like a scientist during our experiment today?
_____
_____
_____
_____
_____
_____
_____

What do you think was the most difficult part of the experiment today? Why?
_____
_____
_____
_____
_____
_____
_____

Could you have done anything differently to get a different outcome? How?
_____
_____
_____
_____
_____
_____
_____

C. Claim, Evidence, Reasoning (CER) Chart

Claim:

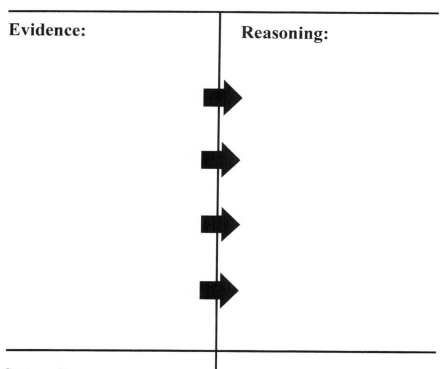

Evidence: # Reasoning:

Sentence Stems:
- The chart shows that...
- Based on the data,
- For example,
- That article states that...
- Another piece of evidence is...

* This is why...
* As a result,
* Because of this,
* This proves that...
* Because...

VOCABULARY ACTIVITIES

A. Heads Up!
B. I Have, Who Has?
C. Bingo Card
D. Vocabulary Chart
E. Definition Chart

A. Heads Up!

This vocabulary activity is based on the popular children's game called Hedbanz by Spin Master Games. The marketed game involves players using a plastic headband that is placed on their forehead. A place on the band is available to hold a card. Because the card is on the person's forehead, they cannot see it but everyone else can. Players give clues to get the person wearing the headband to guess what is on the card. This concept can be applied in any subject with any vocabulary words. Write the vocabulary words on index cards or sticky notes. The first player can grab a card or note and hold it up to their forehead. Make sure that words cannot be seen through the card. Set a timer for one minute to see how many cards the person can successfully guess before the timer goes off. This can be done as a team relay game, individually, or in pairs.

B. I Have, Who Has?

"I have, who has?" is another great game for learning vocabulary, and this one involves the whole class. In this game, each card includes an "I have" statement and a "Who has" question. The first card starts out with "I have the first card"; this helps students to determine who starts the game. Then the first card asks, "Who has . . . ?"; the answer to that question will be on someone else's card. For example, student 1: "I have the first card. Who has a disguise to help blend in or appear hidden?" Student 2: "I have camouflage. Who has a change in a trait that helps an organism survive?" The game play goes on until they reach the last card. For example, student 28: "I have gravity. Who has the first card?" Be sure to include enough vocabulary terms so that every person in the class has a card.

C. Bingo Card

In each box, write a vocabulary word. Listen as the definitions are read, and mark the box with the words that match. The first person to mark all words can shout, "Bingo!"

B	I	N	G	O
★				
		★		
				★

D. Vocabulary Chart

Vocabulary Word	Use in a Sentence	Make a Connection	Illustrate

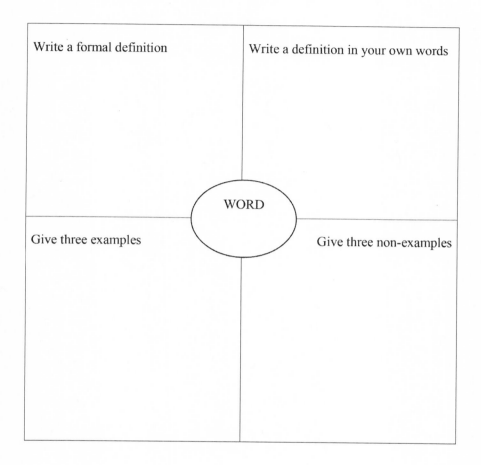

E. Definition Chart

Use this chart to define scientific vocabulary words:

Write a formal definition	Write a definition in your own words
Give three examples	Give three non-examples

WORD

Appendix A
Pancake Chemistry Log

Physical change is when the _____ is changed, but not _____.

Examples: _____

Chemical change is when the _____ have been _____
to change into a new substance.

Examples: _____

Sort the following events used in making pancakes into either a physical or chemical change in the T-chart below.

Physical Change	*Chemical Change*

Measuring flour	Cracking eggs
Mixing milk	Cooking pancakes

Appendix B
Edible Landfill Log

Make a diagram of your model landfill. Draw and label each layer.

Answer the following question after eating your creation and getting to the bottom cookie layer:

Is your bottom-layer "soil" dry, or did the "leachate" ice cream leak through? Explain why you think this occurred.

_____

_____

_____

_____

Appendix C
How Many Ways Do You Taste? Chart

What Flavors Are the Drinks?					
Put an X in the box that matches the flavor to the color.					
	Lemon	*Strawberry*	*Blueberry*	*Apple*	*Orange*
Red Drink					
Yellow Drink					
Blue Drink					
Green Drink					

Answer the following questions in complete sentences:

What did you notice about the different drinks in your tasting cups?

_____

_____

_____

Close your eyes and have a fellow scientist hand you each of the cups to try again. What did you notice when you tried each sample with your eyes closed?

_____

_____

_____

What does this tell you about using your senses as a scientist?

_____

_____

_____

Appendix D
Scientific Method with Bubble Gum

Step 1: Problem—Which brand of bubble gum will blow the biggest bubble?

Step 2: Observation—Name at least three characteristics of each bubble gum.

Bubble Gum Brand A Characteristics	*Bubble Gum Brand B* Characteristics

Step 3: Hypothesis—Write your prediction on which brand will blow the biggest bubble and why. _____

_____

Step 4: Experiment—Follow the steps and complete the chart below.

- Partner 1 chews brand A of bubble gum for three minutes, then blows a bubble.
- Partner 2 uses the string to measure the diameter across the bubble. Place the string on the ruler to measure the distance in centimeters.
- Partner 1 blows two more bubbles and partner 2 measures the diameter of each. Add the numbers together and divide by 3 to get the average.
- Partner 2 chews brand B of bubble gum and follows the steps above with partner 1 doing the measuring.

	Diameter	*Diameter*	*Diameter*	*Average*
Brand A Bubble Gum				
Brand B Bubble Gum				

Step 5: Conclusion—Write your conclusions based on the experiment.

_____

_____

Appendix E

Bird Beaks Investigation Log

Investigate by using each tool to pick up the different types of foods. Record your data in the chart below.

Food	Best Tool (Beak)	Observations
gummy worms		
cooked spaghetti		
rice		
macaroni		
beans		
raisins		
birdseed		
water		

Answer the following questions in complete sentences:

By observing the shape of a bird's beak, what can you infer about the food the bird eats?

_____

_____

Scientists often use models to help them test ideas. How did using models help you test your ideas about bird beaks?

_____

_____

_____

Challenge!: Can you name a bird type that matches each of the bird beak types?

_____

_____

_____

Appendix F
Birds and Worms Recording Log

Record your individual responses below.

Color of round 1 "worm" _____

Color of round 2 "worm" _____

Record class data in the chart below.

Color	*Round 1* (tally for each worm caught)	*Round 2* (tally for each worm caught)

Answer the following questions in complete sentences:

Which color worm was the easiest to find? Which color worm was the hardest to find? Why?

_____

_____

Name a habitat where you think red and yellow worms would blend in more and green and brown worms would stick out.

_____

_____

What color worm would you want to be? Why?

_____

_____

Appendix G
Pipe Cleaner Creature Log

Complete the information for your creature on the chart.

Name of new creature species _____

(Circle one) My creature is a(n)   animal   plant   fungus   bacteria

Creature	
Draw your creature.	Describe your creature (focus on adaptations: coloring, covering, body parts, defense, etc.).
Habitat	
Draw your creature's habitat.	Describe the habitat (biome type, climate, other living/nonliving things).

Answer the following questions in complete sentences:

If you were to do this activity again using the same supplies, how would you change your design to better ensure the survival of your creature?

_____

_____

What different supplies would you use to better ensure the survival of your creature?

_____

_____

Appendix H
Talking Drums Chart

Evaluate the use of drums below as a talking drum. Would each drum make a good talking drum? Why or why not?

Type of Drum	Good Talking Drum?	Why or Why Not?
Snare		
Bass drum		
Tenor		
Timpani		
Congas		
Bongos		
Djembe		

Write out some rhythms and words you created for your talking drum.

Appendix I

Cooking with the Sun
Pre- and Post-Questions

Answer the following questions *before* completing the experiment:

What is the purpose of the aluminum foil?

_____

Why would we use black paper and not another color?

_____

Why do we need the plastic wrap?

_____

Draw the setup of the experiment	
Before taking outside:	After taking outside:

Choose three of the following questions to answer *after* completing the experiment:

How could you make your s'more cook faster?

_____

_____

Do you think it would take the same amount of time to melt four s'mores as it does to melt one?

_____

_____

How do you think this oven would work on an overcast day?

_____

_____

What factors impacted the solar oven the most?

_____

_____

If you could start over, what might you do differently?

_____

_____

Appendix J
Wildlife Scavenger Hunt

Find the items on the list. Place a check mark beside each item found. Collect the items or take a photograph of each.

Item	√	Item	√
Partially nibbled acorn		Animal bone	
Bird feather		Shell from an animal	
Owl pellet		Empty cocoon	
Abandoned bird nest		Animal footprints	
Claw marks on a tree		Piece of animal fur stuck to thorns	
Snail trail		Seed pod	

Answer the questions below in complete sentences:

What animals and insects live nearby? How do you know?

_____

_____

_____

_____

What are some other signs of wildlife that you could look for in this area?

_____

_____

Appendix K
Mystery Powder Table

Use your scientific skills to test properties of each powder. Record your findings in the table below. Try to identify each of the powders after completing all the tests.

Powder	*Observations— What can you tell by looking?*	*Touch— What do you notice by feeling?*	*Smell— What adjectives describe the odor?*	*Solubility— What happens when you experiment with drops of . . .*		
				Water	*Vinegar*	*Iodine*
Powder A						
Powder B						
Powder C						
Powder D						
Powder E						

Identify each of the powders.

Powder A _____

Powder B _____

Powder C _____

Powder D _____

Powder E _____

Appendix L

Water Drops on a Penny Log

Make an observation about the surface of your penny.

_____

_____

Problem: How many drops of water can fit on the surface of a penny?

Estimate: _____

Hypothesis: _____

Use the dropper to add drops to the penny one at a time and tally the number in the chart below.

	Tallies	*Number*
Drops of water on penny		

What conclusions can you draw?

_____

_____

Problem: How many drops of water can fit on the surface of a penny?

Estimate: _____

Hypothesis: _____

Use the dropper to add drops to the penny one at a time. Tally the number of drops in the chart below.

	Tallies	*Number*
Drops of water on penny		

What conclusions can you draw?

_____

_____

If you were to do this experiment again, what liquid would you like to test next? Why? What do you predict would be the results?

_____

_____

Summary of Activities

#	Activity Title	Topic	Vocabulary	Page #
	**Chapter 1: Using Food to Teach Science**			
1	*Pancake Chemistry*	Physical and Chemical Changes with Cooking	physical change, chemical change, gluten	2
2	*Edible Landfill*	Landfills	leachate, decomposition, methane gas, rodent	4
3	*Brown Apples*	Oxidation	oxidized, chemical	5
4	*Pop Rocks and Soda Pop*	Chemistry with Carbon Dioxide	hypothesize, carbon dioxide	6
5	*How Many Ways Do You Taste?*	Sense of Taste	salty, bitter, sweet, savory, sour, flavor	7
6	*Secret Food Codes*	Writing Messages with Food	organic, dilute, consensus	8
7	*Don't Burn the Toast*	Types of Heat Transfer	conduction, convection, radiation	8
8	*Mostly Cloudy*	Types of Clouds	cirrus, cumulus, stratus, nimbus	9
9	*Baking Footprints*	Fossils	paleontologist, fossil	10
10	*Iron for Breakfast*	Iron in Food	dissolve, soluble, fortify	11

#	Activity Title	Topic	Vocabulary	Page #
11	*Eating the Moon*	Phases of the Moon	phase, gibbous, waxing, waning, crescent, counterclockwise, illuminate	12
12	*Milky Magic*	Chemical Changes with Milk	casein	14
13	*Scientific Bubble Gum*	Using the Scientific Method	scientific method	15
Chapter 2: Using Games to Teach Science				
14	*Guess the Scientist*	Famous Scientists	Nobel Prize, obscure	21
15	*Toss the Globe*	Characteristics of Earth	globe, characteristic	22
16	*Bird Beaks*	Animal Adaptations	adaptation	23
17	*Catch Me If You Can*	Habitats	habitat, organism, terrain	24
18	*Rock Scavenger Hunt with GPS*	Types of Rocks	sedimentary, metamorphic, igneous	25
19	*Birds and Worms*	Animal Adaptations	camouflage, adaptation, habitat	25
20	*Pipe Cleaner Camouflage*	Animal Adaptations	biome, adaptation, camouflage, habitat, mimicry	27
21	*Minecraft Science*	Science in Video Games	biome, creeper, nether, mobs, mod, multiplayer, sandbox, skin, spawn, teleport	28
Chapter 3: Using Literature to Teach Science				
22	*Catch a Science Rhyme*	Science in Poetry	life cycle, maturation	33
23	*Constellation Stories*	Star Stories	constellation, celestial coordinates, galaxy, Milky Way, star	34

#	Activity Title	Topic	Vocabulary	Page #
24	*Sky Colors*	Rainbows	horizontal, vertical, prism	36
25	*Universe of Reading*	Space in Books	asteroid, meteor, light-year, black hole	37
26	*Sci-Fi Reality*	Aliens and UFOs	UFO, phenomena, science fiction, alien, extraterrestrial, AI, dystopian, postapocalyptic, propaganda, surveillance, cyborg, android	38
Chapter 4: Using Music to Teach Science				
27	*Sing a Song of Science*	Science in Music	tune, tempo, rhythm	43
28	*Good Vibrations*	Music Vibrations	vibration, treble clef, bass clef	44
29	*Pitch Perfect*	Music Pitch	pitch, range, harmony, harmonic interval, tone, scale	45
30	*Broadway and Science*	Science in Music	genre, improvisation, projection, callback, dress rehearsals, downstage	47
31	*Talking Drums*	Communication through Drumming	percussion, rhythm, pitch	48
Chapter 5: Using the Community and the Natural Environment to Teach Science				
32	*Ruining an Ecosystem*	Ecosystems	ecosystem, wetland, old-growth forest, biodiversity	56
33	*Spinning, Whirling, Dripping*	Weather Measurement	thermometer, anemometer, wind vane, rain gauge, barometer	58

#	Activity Title	Topic	Vocabulary	Page #
34	*What Poop Is That?*	Identifying Scat	scatologist, scat	59
35	*Cooking with the Sun*	Solar Oven	solar radiation, greenhouse effect	60
36	*We're Going to the Zoo, How about You?*	Zoo Scavenger Hunt	captivity, adaptation, carnivorous, endangered, habitat, mammal, nocturnal, amphibian	61
37	*Million-Dollar Property*	Point and Nonpoint Source Pollutants	point source pollution, nonpoint source pollution	63
38	*Natural Treasures*	Wildlife Scavenger Hunt	camouflage, naturalist	64
Chapter 6: Using Everyday Objects to Teach Science				
39	*Telling Time with Shadows*	Sundials	gnomon, latitude, true north, hemisphere, solar time	68
40	*Body Molecules*	Potential and Kinetic Energy	molecules, kinetic energy, potential energy	69
41	*Picture This: Science*	Science with Photography	foreground, background, composition, contrast, exposure	70
42	*Lights! Action! Science!*	Science in Film	B movie, genre, cosmos, interstellar, terraforming	71
43	*Pulp and Paper*	Making Paper	opaque, transparent, cellulose, recycle	73
44	*Salt and Water*	Freezing Point of Water	Celsius, Fahrenheit, adhere, ions	75

#	Activity Title	Topic	Vocabulary	Page #
45	*All Charged Up*	Static Electricity	levitate, electron, proton, static electricity	76
46	*Can You Take the Pressure?*	Air Pressure	air pressure, barometer, atmosphere	77
47	*Penny for Your Force*	Centripetal Force	force, centripetal force, centrifugal force, tether, inertia	79
48	*Mystery Powder*	Identifying Unknown Substances	solubility, physical property, chemical property	80
49	*Foam Alone*	Making a Fire Extinguisher	extinguish, retardant	81
50	*Water Drops on a Penny*	Surface Tension	hypothesis, surface tension, variable	82

Bibliography

Andrews, Kim. *Exploring Nature: Activity Book for Kids*. Emeryville, CA: Rockridge, 2019.

Ardley, Neil. *101 Great Science Experiments*. New York: Dorling Kindersley, 1993.

Bachiorri, Antonella, Paola Bortolon, Maria Angela Fontechiari, Frankie McKeon, and Anna Pascucci. *Everyday Objects: Linking IBSE and ESD*. UK: Lifelong Learning Programme of the European Union, 2016. Accessed May 18, 2022. https://fondation-lamap.org/sites/default/files/upload/media/minisites/sustain/Everyday _objects_handbook.pdf.

Bintz, William P., Pam Wright, and Julie Sheffer. "Using Copy Change with Trade Books to Teach Earth Science." *Reading Teacher* 64, no. 2 (2010): 106–19.

Craven, Kathryn S., Alex Collier, and Jay Y. S. Hodgson. "Spiders by Night: An Outdoor Investigation Integrating Next Generation Science Standards." *American Biology Teacher* 81, no. 8 (2019): 561–67.

Crowther, Gregory. "Using Science Songs to Enhance Learning: An Interdisciplinary Approach." *Life Sciences Education* 11, no. 1 (2012): 26–30.

DeMetz, Kay. "Toward a Synthesis of Science and Theatre Arts." *Forum on Public Policy* 2007, no. 1 (2007): 1–13.

DeSouza, Josephine M. Shireen. "Nature Teaches: Young Children's Experiences Learning Science Outdoors." In *Science Education Research and Practice in Asia-Pacific and Beyond*, edited by Jennifer Yeo, Tang Wee Teo, and Kok-Sing Tang. Singapore: Springer, 2018. https://doi.org/10.1007/978-981-10-5149-4_8.

Environmental Protection Agency (EPA). *A Teacher's Guide to Reducing, Reusing, and Recycling: The Quest for Less (Activities and Resources for Teaching K–8)*. Washington, DC: Environmental Protection Agency, 2005.

Gardner, Martin. *Entertaining Science Experiments with Everyday Objects*. New York: Dover, 1981.

Gates, Stefan. *Science You Can Eat*. New York: DK, 2019.

Greenspan, Yvette F. *A Guide to Teaching Elementary Science: Ten Easy Steps*. Boston: Sense, 2016.

Honey, Margaret A., and Margaret Hilton, eds. *Learning Science through Computer Games and Simulations*. Washington, DC: National Academies Press, 2011.

Kaser, Sandy. "Searching the Heavens with Children's Literature: A Design for Teaching Science." *Language Arts* 78, no. 4 (2001): 348–56.

Kersten, Sara. "Becoming Nonfiction Authors: Engaging in Science Inquiry." *Reading Teacher* 71, no. 1 (2017): 33–41. https://doi.org/10.1002/trtr.1577.

McCarthy, Deborah. "Straws and Air Pressure: Using an Everyday Object to Explain Air Pressure." *Science Scope* 37, no. 8 (2014): 23–28.

Project Learning Tree. *Project Learning Tree Pre K–8 Environmental Education Activity Guide*. 4th ed. Washington, DC: Sustainable Forestry Initiative, 2019.

Riendeau, Diane. "Using the Real World to Teach Physics." *Physics Teacher* 52, no. 2 (2014): 125. https://doi.org/10.1119/1.4862128.

Roberts, J. L., and J. R. Boggess, *Teacher's Survival Guide: Gifted Education.* Waco, TX: Prufrock, 2011.

Rogers, George L. "The Music of the Spheres: Cross-Curricular Perspectives on Music and Science." *National Association for Music Education* 103, no. 1 (2016): 41–48. https://doi.org/10.1177/0027432116654547.

Rousu, Matthew C. "Using Show Tunes to Teach about Free (and Not-So-Free) Markets." *Journal of Private Enterprise* 33, no. 4 (2018): 111–28.

Royce, Christine Anne, Emily Morgan, and Karen Ansberry. *Teaching Science through Trade Books*. Arlington, VA: National Science Teachers Association, 2012.

Seefeldt, Carol. "Teaching Science through the Visual Arts and Music." *Scholastic Early Childhood Today* 18, no. 6 (2004): 29–34.

Short, Dan Brian. "Teaching Scientific Concepts Using a Virtual World—Minecraft." *Teaching Science* 58, no. 3 (2012): 55–58.

Southwest Educational Development Laboratory. "Using Community Resources." *Classroom Compass* 3, no. 1 (1996): 1–3, 10.

Spangler, Steve. *10-Minute Science Experiments*. New York: Topix Media Lab, 2019.

Tymony, Cy. *Sneaky Uses for Everyday Things*. Kansas City, MO: Andrews McMeel, 2020.

Western Regional Environmental Education Council. *Project Wet: Curriculum and Activity Guide*. Bozeman, MT: The Watercourse, and Houston, TX: Western Regional Environmental Education Council, 1995.

Williamson, Keith M., Lee Land, Beverly Butler, and Hassan B. Ndahi. "A Structured Framework for Using Games to Teach Mathematics and Science in K–12 Classrooms." *Technology Teacher* 64, no. 5 (2004): 15–18.

Worch, Eric A., Amy M. Scheuermann, and Jodi J. Haney. "Role-Play in the Science Classroom." *Science and Children* 47, no. 1 (2009): 54–59.

Worth, Karen. "Science in Early Childhood Classrooms: Content and Process." *Early Childhood Research & Practice (ECRP)* 12, no. 2 (2010): 1–17.

About the Authors and Illustrator

ABOUT THE AUTHORS

Dr. **S. Kay Gandy** was an elementary teacher of twenty-seven years in Louisiana, and a university professor of seventeen years in Kentucky. She currently is self-employed as an education consultant and resides in Arkansas. Dr. Gandy is a perpetual student and has five degrees from three universities. She is the author of *Mapping Is Elementary, My Dear: 100 Activities to Teach Map Skills to K–6 Students* and *50 Ways to Teach Social Studies for Elementary Teachers*. One of her passions is international education, and she has created many opportunities for both faculty and students to travel abroad. She has received two Fulbright awards to South Africa and one to Senegal and has planned study abroad trips for faculty and students to Peru, England, and Costa Rica. She has worked extensively with teachers from China and led social studies presentations and workshops for teachers in New Zealand, South Africa, Spain, England, Chile, and Scotland.

Harmony Hendrick is an elementary school teacher in Kentucky. She has both bachelor's and master's degrees and is currently finishing her Rank 1 with Gifted Endorsement. She has been teaching for the past sixteen years in fourth and fifth grades. She has worked with national and local organizations to present dynamic lessons for teachers.

Jessica Roberts is a fifth-generation educator and has been an elementary teacher for the past seventeen years in Kentucky. She has both bachelor's and master's degrees in elementary education. She has developed teacher resources and shared presentations nationally.

135

ABOUT THE ILLUSTRATOR

Madalyn Stack is a graphic designer and illustrator from Louisville, Kentucky. She is a graduate of Western Kentucky University and currently works as a medical illustrator in Louisville. Ms. Stack illustrated the book covers and cartoons for *Mapping Is Elementary, My Dear: 100 Activities to Teach Map Skills to K–6 Students* and *50 Ways to Teach Social Studies for Elementary Teachers*.